THE

SUNDAY SCHOOL CONCERT,

A

GENERAL SERVICE MANUAL;

FOR THE

SCHOOL AND CONGREGATION.

BY THE SUPERINTENDENT AND TEACHERS OF THE CONG'L SUNDAY SCHOOL, WINONA, MINN.

CHICAGO:
ADAMS, BLACKMER, & LYON PUBLISHING CO.
1872.

Electrotyped by A. ZEESE & Co.,
17 N. Jefferson St., Chicago.

DEDICATION.

TO SUNDAY SCHOOL TEACHERS

EVERYWHERE, WHOSE

SELF-DENYING AND FAITHFUL LABORS OF LOVE

HAVE BEEN

SO RICHLY BLESSED BY THE HOLY SPIRIT

IN THE SALVATION OF SOULS, AS WELL AS IN THE

GREAT WORK OF MAKING THE PRINCIPLES OF GOD'S WORD

THE CONTROLLING POWER IN THE LAND,

THIS VOLUME IS AFFECTIONATELY INSCRIBED.

CONTENTS.

INTRODUCTION.

CONCERNING THE SUNDAY SCHOOL AND THE SUNDAY SCHOOL CONCERT.—OBJECTS AND ADVANTAGES OF THE SUNDAY SCHOOL CONCERT.—CHARACTER OF THE EXERCISE; AS TO ITS SUBJECT-MATTER, DISTINCTIVE FEATURES, TIME AND FREQUENCY, IMMEDIATE PREPARATION AND CONDUCT, ... 11

SUNDAY SCHOOL CONCERT EXERCISES.

I.

THE BIBLE:

A LESSON CONCERNING GOD'S REVELATION TO MAN, . 21

II.

ABRAHAM:

A LESSON OF PROMISE, ... 31

III.

ABRAHAM:

A LESSON OF FAITH, ... 45

IV.

MOSES,

THE EGYPTIAN, THE EXILE, THE LEADER:

A Lesson of God in History, ... 57

V.

ISAIAH:

A Lesson of Christ in Prophecy, ... 71

VI.

THE MOUNTAINS OF THE BIBLE:

A Lesson Concerning the Earthly Scenes of God's Glory, ... 85

VII.

PRAYER:

A Lesson of Devotion, ... 99

VIII.

OUR SAVIOUR:

A Lesson for Christmas, ... 109

IX.

THE LORD'S PRAYER:

A Lesson for Every Day in the Year, ... 121

X.

THE SERMON ON THE MOUNT:

A Lesson from the Words of Christ, ... 131

XI.

AROUND GENNESARET:

A Lesson from the Life of Christ, ... 141

XII.

CHRIST THE FOUNDATION STONE:

A Lesson concerning "Living Stones" in "God's Building," 153

XIII.

THE NAME OF JESUS:

A Lesson from the Titles of Christ, ... 165

XIV.

CHRIST TO THE CHURCHES:

A Lesson of Warning and Promise, ... 175

XV.

THE CROSS AND THE CROWN:

A Lesson of Salvation, ... 189

XVI.

ANGELS:

A Lesson Concerning Heavenly Things, ... 201

XVII.

OUR HEAVENLY HOME:

A Lesson of Victory, ... 213

APPENDIX.

THE GENERAL EXERCISES: THEIR CHARACTER AND IMPORTANCE; PRAYER — READING — SINGING, ETC., ... 227

SELECTIONS, RESPONSES, CHANTS, ETC.

I.

SELECTIONS.

AN OPENING EXERCISE — PRAYER — GO WHEN THE MORNING SHINETH — TWENTY-THIRD PSALM — LOVING SHEPHERD — THE LORD WILL PROVIDE — HOW CAN A CHILD BE SAVED? — THE OLD, OLD STORY—THE CROSS PRESENTED — THE WAY OF THE CROSS THE WAY OF LIGHT — THE SEA OF GALILEE — JERUSALEM THE GOLDEN — BEAUTIFUL THINGS ABOVE — THE QUEEN'S DECISION — THE MOUNTAINS OF THE BIBLE — OUR WORK IS HERE, 231

II.

RESPONSIVE READINGS.

PSALMS I, VII, XXIV, XC, CIII, CXIX: 97–128, CXXV, ISAIAH XI: 1–9, IV: 1–7—THE BEATITUDES—THE APOSTLES' CREED, ... 244

III.

CHANTS.

THE LORD'S PRAYER — THE SAVIOUR — GLORIA PATRI — PSALM XCVI — PSALM XIX — LUKE II — PRAISE THE LORD — BLESSED BE THE LORD GOD OF ISRAEL — OH COME, LET US SING — GOD BE MERCIFUL — THE LORD IS MY SHEPHERD — THE INVITATION — I WILL LIFT UP MINE EYES — HAPPY HOME (Song), ... 252

INTRODUCTION.

Concerning the Sunday School and the Sunday School Concert.

The present and the future of the Sunday-school is, to the Christian mind of to-day, a matter of vast importance. Although there is a "hopeful discontent with the present state of things" in this department of Christian work, yet there is much to be thankful for, and much to make the future hopeful in the general advancement of the study of God's word through the Sunday-school. There is now, more than formerly, a skillful adaptation of means to an end, and the fact has come to be recognized that the "Lord's business" requires the consecration of *mind* as well as of *heart*—that he blesses intellect and genius when employed in his service. We cannot fail to mark an increased interest in the general work of the church on the part of the laity, and the extensive application of improved methods of instruction in the Sunday-school. Books and periodical literature, appliances and apparatus, have been multiplied to meet the demand for them until we have been almost in danger of forgetting the end of our toil in admiration of the means. But the truths of the Bible are brought, in an attractive and comprehensive form, to all classes of scholars.

Among the special means of improvement we may notice two, as having led the way and made others possible. These have been, first, the *topical method* of instruction in the Scriptures; and second, the *uniform lesson system*. The latter has been adopted by so great a number of schools as to render it possible to sustain an able periodical literature largely for the purpose of developing these lessons for both teachers and pupils of all grades in the school. We can now rejoice in the fact that a vast array of talent, comprising many of the ablest minds of the country, is now engaged in this noble work.

Great credit is due to the pioneers in the enterprise of the topical and uniform lesson system.

Let it now be the earnest prayer and constant effort of every Christian, that the hearts of the youth of the land may be sanctified by the indwelling of God's Spirit, while their minds are enlightened through these instrumentalities of moral and religious culture. "Our intellects," Dr. R. D. Hitchcock once said, "left to work alone, chill out the life principle, the true essence of piety. It is sending the flocks of religious affections up from the genial valleys to perish in Alpine snow."

The Sunday School Concert, or General Service Exercise, has been for many years an important feature of the Sunday-school work. And here progress has been manifest. The old concert, with its speech-making and story-telling, with its want of system and definiteness of purpose, so far as instruction was concerned, was quite in keeping with the random and often irrelevant conversation that formerly constituted most of the Bible-class work —we can hardly say instruction—as well as with the meaningless recitation of texts, so often the order of the lower classes. Nevertheless, the old school and the old concert were productive of great good. The spirit of true progress neither ignores the good things of the past nor rests contented with the imperfections of the present.

It is humbly hoped that this little work will prove to be, not merely a manual of *Concert Exercises*, but a contribution toward the development of the true ideal of what this service should be.

I.

Objects and Advantages of the Sunday School Concert.

1. It should be the aim of this exercise to afford *a pleasing variety* in methods of Biblical instruction. All practical teachers recognize the importance of this in securing the attention and interest of the young.

2. It should exhibit great and fundamental truths, the outlines of Scripture, in a manner calculated to *fix them in the memory*, and should so address them to the mind and heart as to make a permanent impression. The general review is to the scholar the most important lesson of the term.

3. The concert exercise should be not only a lesson of instruction, but most emphatically a *service of devotion*. It should always be characterized by religious warmth and fervor. Mr. Beecher recently said: "Among the members of our churches there are ten who are conscientious while there is one who is devout. * * * The coldness of religious feeling, which is so conspicuous a defect in Protestant churches, is largely due to the failure of those churches to make suitable provision for worship in their services."

4. The concert, through the interest of its exercise, may be made a means of leading persons not connected with the school to become attendants upon its regular exercises and upon the services of the church.

II.

What should be the Character of the Concert Exercise?

1. AS TO SUBJECT-MATTER.

There should be one central topic, and the Scripture recitations, the songs, and all the selections should have a bearing upon and cluster around this one central truth. We cannot critically examine the whole Scripture, even in the Sunday-school proper, much less in these less-frequently recurring concert services. Dr. Huntington has truly said: "The life of a child—certainly his Sunday-school life—is far too short for the microscopic study of the Scriptures. Much is accomplished if he be made acquainted with the great outlines of the word of God." There are, both in the Old and New Testaments, prominent characters and great central truths, by the study of which we may comprehend, so far as we are able, not only these, but much that lies between and clusters around them. Abraham, Moses, and Isaiah, are representatives of such characters, and around them and a few others we associate the great facts, historical and prophetic, concerning God's ancient dispensation. The advent, life and death of the Saviour, as given by the evangelists, his own teachings, as in the sermon on the mount, the preaching of Paul, and the heavenly vision of the Revelator, are among the great facts of the gospel of the New Testament. These great truths of prophecy, history, and revelation, make up the grand outline of God's word. These are the "Mountains of the Bible," eternal and immovable, from whose lofty summits we may get glimpses of the realms of God's truth extending like a limitless ocean beyond our mental vision, and from whose heights the eye of faith may sometimes behold dim outlines of the celestial country.

2. AS TO THE DISTINCTIVE FEATURES OF THE EXERCISE.

Let it be interesting, instructive, devotional, *never theatrical.* Let the lesson, not the actors, be the object of interest. Too much of ordinary dialogue and declamation are not in accordance with the spirit of devotion, and are out of place in the service of the church and Sunday-school. Let the Sunday-school concert never be degraded to a mere exhibition of smart children. To avoid even the appearance of this, as well as that a greater number may feel a personal interest in the meeting, the superintendent should, as far as possible, avoid assigning prominent parts to the same pupils on successive occasions. Even the parts of the little ones, brought in from the infant department to give variety and completeness to the whole, should have some connection with the main idea of the lesson.

3. AS TO TIME AND FREQUENCY.

The concert should not be held too often, lest so much of the time and attention of the school be taken for preparation work as to encroach upon the regular study and work of the school; yet often enough to afford that variety of exercise, and to maintain that healthful stimulus which it is the object of the concert to give to the school. Some schools succeed in having a concert every month, while others find six weeks or two months often enough to secure good and well performed exercises. No other than good performances should ever be allowed. When held, this meeting should not supersede, but rather be the evening service of the church. The Sunday-school is only a department of the work of the church, and should not be regarded as a separate activity. Nor is the Sunday-school for the young only. The concert service should be largely attended by the adult congregation, and, to this end, the exercise should be made interesting and profitable enough to secure such attendance. Let the school acquire and maintain the reputation of never having a poor concert, and the simple announcement of the meeting will secure the audience. The good results of such a course will not alone rest upon the multitude, but the general enthusiasm will react to the interest and great advantage of the school also. The principle holds here, as in all Christian work,—we benefit ourselves most when we most seek to benefit others.

4. AS TO THE IMMEDIATE PREPARATION OF AND HOW TO CONDUCT THE EXERCISE.

The service, to be most successful, should be varied; hence only general directions can be given.

The superintendent should himself assign the parts to the teachers or scholars at least one week beforehand. Teachers may hear their classes rehearse privately, but there should be no general rehearsal of the school. This would detract from the freshness and interest of the exercise at its performance. Care should be taken that assignments are made only to such as can be relied upon for their presence. A few broken links will spoil the chain of instruction, and injure the effect of the lesson. The superintendent conducts the service, having previously made himself thoroughly familiar with the whole exercise; having, at the same time, the copy in hand. Have everything ready before beginning, and have no delays between the exercises; nor any departure from the programme to accommodate any speech-maker who accidentally may be present. The order should be perfect, and every recitation heard and understood by the whole audience. Let the machinery be such as to work silently and unseen; and let it be impelled by love.

Such a discipline can only be obtained, in most schools, by patient effort. The superintendent is the source of the discipline of the school. He must possess peculiar qualities of head and heart; and, moreover, in assuming the duties of his office he must feel that he is committed to the performance of much prayerful, thoughtful, and patient labor for Christ. The Lord's work is worth doing well, and the reward is both *here* and *beyond.*

CONCERT EXERCISES.

I.

The Bible:

A LESSON CONCERNING GOD'S REVELATION TO MAN.

"All scripture is given by inspiration of God."—2 *Tim.* 3: 16.

"Thy word is a lamp unto my feet, and a light unto my path."
—*Ps.* 119: 105.

EXERCISE.

Opening Song. "The Word of the Lord."—Fresh Laurels, p. 41.

Superintendent. "O how love I thy law! it is my meditation all the day."

School. "Thy word is a lamp unto my feet, and a light unto my path."

Chant. "Blessed be the Lord God of Israel."
(*See Appendix.*)

PRAYER.

Scripture Reading. Psalm 119: 1–18.

Singing. "Blessed Bible."—Notes of Joy, p. 11 (or substitute).*

RECITATION.

A little girl repeats from the platform, in a clear voice:

THE BIBLE.

'Tis a pure and holy word,
'Tis the wisdom of a God:
'Tis a fountain full and free,
'Tis the book for you and me:
'Twill the soul's best anchor be
Over life's tempestuous sea;
A guardian angel to the tomb,
A meteor in the world's dark gloom:
'Tis a shining sun at even,
'Tis a diamond dropped from heaven.

* Hymns appropriately selected from the book in use in the school may be substituted, if more convenient, for those designated in these Exercises.

CLASS A.

Supt. What does the Bible claim to be?

Teacher. The word of God—

"For this cause also thank we God without ceasing, because, when ye received the word of God which ye heard of us, ye received it not as the word of men, but, as it is in truth, the word of God, which effectually worketh also in you that believe." —1 Thess. 2: 13.

Supt. Do the Old and New Testaments differ as to authority?

First Pupil. "God, who at sundry times and in divers manners spake in time past unto the fathers by the prophets, hath in these last days spoken unto us by his Son."—Heb. 1: 1, 2.

Supt. How long before Christ were the books of Moses written?

Second Pupil. About 1,450 years.

Supt. And yet do their teachings harmonize with the gospel of Christ?

Third Pupil. "Had ye believed Moses, ye would have believed me: for he wrote of me."—John 5: 46.

Supt. To what great truth do all the teachings of both the Old and New Testaments point?

Fourth Pupil. "To him give all the prophets witness, that through his name whosoever believeth in him shall receive remission of sins."—Acts 10: 43.

Fifth Pupil. "Saying none other things than those which the prophets and Moses did say should come: that Christ should suffer, and that he should be the first that should rise from the dead, and should shew light unto the people, and to the Gentiles."—Acts 26: 22, 23.

Singing. From "New Golden Shower," p. 98.

1 O Lord, thy perfect word
Directs our steps aright,
Nor can all other books afford
Such profit and delight.

2 Celestial beams it sheds
 To cheer this vale below:
To distant lands its glory spreads,
 And streams of mercy flow.

3 True wisdom it imparts,
 Commands our hope and fear:
Oh, may we hide it in our hearts,
 And feel its influence there.

CLASS B.

Supt. How was the Law first given to man?

First Pupil. "And the Lord said unto Moses, Come up to me into the mount, and be there: and I will give thee tables of stone, and a law, and commandments which I have written; that thou mayest teach them."—Ex. 24: 12.

Second Pupil. "And he gave unto Moses, when he had made an end of communing with him upon mount Sinai, two tables of testimony, tables of stone, written with the finger of God."—Ex. 31: 18.

Supt. Where do we first read of the Law being written in a roll or book?

Third Pupil. "And Moses wrote this law, and delivered it unto the priests the sons of Levi, which bare the ark of the covenant of the Lord, and unto all the elders of Israel."—Deut. 31: 9.

Fourth Pupil. "And it came to pass, when Moses had made an end of writing the words of this law in a book, until they were finished, that Moses commanded the Levites, which bare the ark of the covenant of the Lord, saying, Take this book of the law, and put it in the side of the ark of the covenant of the Lord your God, that it may be there for a witness against thee."—Deut. 31: 24, 25, 26.

Supt. What does Paul say of the Law?

Fifth Pupil. "But before faith came, we were kept under the law, shut up unto the faith which should afterwards be revealed. Wherefore the law was our school-master to bring us unto Christ, that we might be justified by faith."—Gal. 3: 23, 24.

Class C.

Supt. What was the mission of the *prophets?*

Teacher. *" By a long course of teaching, the prophets led the world on until it was fit for Christ; so fit, that when Christ came, the news of his mission was rapidly carried throughout the world, and found acceptance in every city. Even in the Gentile world, at all the great centres of human activity, devout men had been gathered from among the heathen in readiness for Christ. Without being Jews, they went on the Sabbath to the synagogue to hear the words of the prophets read there. These were the men who made Antioch the second mother of the faith, and who gave there to Christianity its name. They were the fruits of prophecy."

These are the words of the prophet Isaiah:

" The voice of him that crieth in the wilderness, Prepare ye the way of the Lord, make straight in the desert a highway for our God."—Is. 40: 3.

Supt. What are some of the texts given in the Old and New Testaments testifying to their inspiration?

First Pupil. " Now these be the last words of David. David the son of Jesse said, and the man who was raised up on high, the anointed of the God of Jacob, and the sweet psalmist of Israel, said, The Spirit of the Lord spake by me, and his word was in my tongue."—2 Sam. 23: 1, 2.

Second Pupil. "And the Lord spake by his servants the prophets, saying."—2 Kings 21: 10.

Third Pupil. " Which things also we speak, not in the words which man's wisdom teacheth, but which the Holy Ghost teacheth; comparing spiritual things with spiritual."—1 Cor. 2: 13.

Fourth Pupil. " But I certify you, brethren, that the gospel which was preached of me is not after man. For I neither received it of man, neither was I taught it, but by the revelation of Jesus Christ."—Gal. 1: 11, 12.

Fifth Pupil. " All Scripture is given by inspiration of God, and is profitable for doctrine, for reproof, for correction, for instruction in righteousness."—1 Tim. 3: 16.

* The prose quotations of this exercise are from the Bampton Lectures, by R. Payne Smith.

Sixth Pupil. "Knowing this first, that no prophecy of the Scripture is of any private interpretation. For the prophecy came not in old time by the will of man: but holy men of God spake as they were moved by the Holy Ghost."—2 Peter 1: 20, 21.

Singing. From "Sabbath Songs," p. 103.

THE BOOK DIVINE.

1 How precious is the Book divine,
By inspiration given!
Bright as a lamp its pages shine,
To guide our souls to heaven.

2 It sweetly cheers our drooping hearts
In this dark vale of tears;
Life, light, and joy it still imparts,
And quells our rising fears.

3 This lamp, through all the tedious night
Of life, shall guide our way,
Till we behold the clearer light
Of an eternal day.

RECITATION.

1 Engraved as in eternal brass
The mighty promise shines;
Nor can the powers of darkness rase
Those everlasting lines.

2 The sacred word of grace is strong
As that which built the skies;
The voice which rolls the stars along
Spake all the promises.

3 My hiding place, my refuge, tower,
And shield art thou, O Lord!
I firmly anchor all my hopes
On thine unerring word. *Watts.*

CLASS D.

Supt. Will a hasty reading of the Bible reveal all its truths?

First Pupil. "Search the Scriptures; for in them ye think ye have eternal life: and they are they which testify of me."—John 5: 39.

Second Pupil. "These were more noble than those in Thessalonica, in that they received the word with all readiness of mind, and searched the Scriptures daily, whether those things were so."—Acts 17: 11.

Supt. What blessings result from a love for and careful study of the Bible?

Third Pupil. "The entrance of thy words giveth light; it giveth understanding unto the simple."—Ps. 119: 130.

Fourth Pupil. "I have rejoiced in the way of thy testimonies, as much as in all riches."—Ps. 119: 14.

Fifth Pupil. "Unless thy law had been my delight, I should have perished in mine affliction."—Ps. 119: 92.

Sixth Pupil. "Wherewithal shall a young man cleanse his way? by taking heed thereto according to thy word."—Ps. 119: 9.

Seventh Pupil. "For whatsoever things were written aforetime were written for our learning, that we through patience and comfort of the Scriptures might have hope."—Rom. 15: 4.

Eighth Pupil. "For I am not ashamed of the gospel of Christ: for it is the power of God unto salvation to every one that believeth; to the Jew first, and also to the Greek."—Rom. 1: 16.

Supt. "Faith is best established in the heart by the *close study* of the Bible. If it be God's book, it will speak best in God's behalf. It must carry its proof with it. Such a proof is found in the unity and consistency of the Bible, and the wonderful way in which its many treatises form one book, all combining in setting before men one and the same way provided by God for man's restoration. In the Bible, men find the same plan of salvation gradually and steadily unfolded. It grows more plain, more clear and definite as speaker after speaker arises with words from God. No one ever contradicts the past, but each adds his own measure of truth to that already given. And finally—It is finished—the message of God to the soul is completed under such circumstances, and with so great an outpouring of Divine light, as infinitely to excel, while nevertheless it fulfills and exactly corresponds to all the previous declarations of the prophets.

"And then the most convincing evidence of all is our Lord's own character. The more we study that simple but marvelous delineation of him given in the gospel, the more certain we feel of his unapproachable perfectness; that no man ever spake as he spake, or taught as he taught, or wrought as he wrought."

RECITATION.

THE BIBLE.

1 Thank God for the Bible! 'tis there that we find
The story of Christ and his love —
How he came down to earth, from his beautiful home
In the mansions of glory above;
Thanks to him we will bring,
Praise to him we will sing,
For he came down to earth, from his beautiful home
In the mansions of glory above.

2 While he lived on this earth, to the sick and the blind,
And to mourners, his blessings were given;
And he said, Let the little ones come unto me,
For of such is the kingdom of heaven.
Jesus calls us to come,
He's prepared us a home,
For he said, Let the little ones come unto me,
For of such is the kingdom of heaven.

3 In the Bible we read of a beautiful land,
Where sorrow and pain never come;
For Jesus is there with a heavenly band,
And 'tis there he's prepared us a home.
Jesus calls, shall we stay?
No! we'll gladly obey,
For Jesus is there with a heavenly band,
And 'tis there he's prepared us a home.

4 Thank God for the Bible! its truths o'er the earth
We'll scatter with a bountiful hand;
But we never can tell what a Bible is worth,
Till we go to that beautiful land.
There our thanks we'll bring,
There with angels we'll sing,
And its worth we can tell, when with Jesus we dwell,
In heaven — that beautiful land.

Singing. From "The Silver Song," p. 48 — duet and chorus.

THE BIBLE.

1 What is it points my soul the way
To realms of everlasting day,
And tells the danger of delay?
It is the precious Bible.

CHORUS.— The Bible, the Bible,
The precious, precious Bible;
It points the way to heaven above,
The precious, precious Bible.

2 What teaches me that I must love
The glorious God who reigns above,
And that I may his glories prove?
It is the precious Bible.

CHORUS.

3 What is it gives my spirit rest,
When with the cares of earth oppressed,
And points to regions of the blest?
It is the precious Bible.

CHORUS.

CLASS E.

Supt. Will all who listen to Bible truths be saved?

First Pupil. "Now the parable is this: The seed is the word of God, Those by the way side are they that hear; then cometh the devil, and taketh away the word out of their hearts, lest they should believe and be saved."— Luke 8: 11, 12.

Second Pupil. "They on the rock are they, which, when they hear, receive the word with joy; and these have no root, which for a while believe, and in time of temptation fall away."— Luke 8: 13.

Third Pupil. "And that which fell among thorns are they, which, when they have heard, go forth, and are choked with cares and riches and pleasures of this life, and bring no fruit to perfection."— Luke 8: 14.

Fourth Pupil. "But that on the good ground are they, which in an honest and good heart, having heard the word, keep it, and bring forth fruit with patience."— Luke 8: 15.

Teacher. "Take heed therefore, how ye hear."—Luke 8: 18, first clause.

Supt. Comparing Christian with heathen lands, where the Bible is unknown, what difference do we find?

Teacher. "In proportion as men study the Bible and act upon it, they become more just, more temperate, more self-denying, more willing to labor for the good of others. Destroy this book, and the bond between rich and poor is gone. There is nothing to speak to both alike of a God who is no respecter of persons. The suffering Christ, the Man of Sorrows, the cross meekly borne, leading onward to the immortal crown—there will be nought of this to comfort the afflicted. The glorified Christ, coming with all power as judge of quick and dead, and in that judgment putting the poor into his own place—there will be nought of this to bid the rich man seek out the poor, and minister to him. To eat and drink and die will be man's all."

Singing. "Happy Voices," p. 72.

We won't give up the Bible,
God's holy book of truth.

CLASS F.

Supt. Are there any to whom God's message is not addressed?

First Pupil. "Come near, ye nations, to hear; and hearken ye people: let the earth hear, and all that is therein: the world, and all things that come forth of it."—Is. 34: 1.

Second Pupil. "He that hath an ear, let him hear what the Spirit saith unto the churches."—Rev. 2: 29.

RECITATION.

1 Holy Bible, book divine,
Precious treasure, thou art mine;
Mine to tell me whence I came;
Mine to teach me what I am:

2 Mine to chide me when I rove;
Mine to show a Saviour's love;
Mine art thou, to guide my youth
In the paths of love and truth:

3 Mine to comfort in distress,
If the Holy Spirit bless,
Mine to show by living faith,
Man can triumph over death:

4 Mine to tell of joys to come,
And the sinner's dreadful doom:
O thou precious book divine;
Precious treasure, thou art mine.

Supt. We all have this precious book. We read and listen to its truths. What yet remains for us to do?

Third Pupil. "Be ye doers of the word, and not hearers only, deceiving your own selves."—James 1: 22.

Fourth Pupil. "Blessed is he that readeth, and they that hear the words of this prophecy, and keep those things which are written therein: for the time is at hand."—Rev. 1: 3.

Ass't Supt. repeats impressively—

Most wondrous book! bright candle of the Lord! star of eternity! the only star by which the barque of man could navigate the sea of life, and gain the coast of bliss securely.

CLOSING HYMN.

ZION.

1 O'er the gloomy hills of darkness,
Cheered by no celestial ray,
Sun of righteousness arising,
Bring the bright, the glorious day;
Send the gospel
To the earth's remotest bound.

2 Kingdoms wide that sit in darkness,
Grant them, Lord, the glorious light;
And from eastern coast to western,
May the morning chase the night,
And redemption,
Freely purchased, win the day.

3 Fly abroad, thou mighty gospel;
Win and conquer—never cease!
May thy lasting, wide dominions
Multiply, and still increase:
Sway thy sceptre,
Saviour, all the world around!

II.

Abraham:

A LESSON OF PROMISE.

"For all the promises of God in him are yea, and in him Amen unto the glory of God by us."—2 *Cor.* 1: 20.

"The Lord is not slack concerning his promises."—2 *Peter* 3: 19.

EXERCISE.

Opening Song. "Come, join our Band."—Fresh Laurels, p. 98.

1 We're marching to the promised land,
  A land all fair and bright;
Come, join our happy, youthful band,
  And seek the plains of light.

   CHORUS—O come, come, come,
  Our glorious songs of triumph share;
We soon shall reach the heavenly land,
  And rest forever there.

2 In that bright land no sin is found,
  For all are happy, happy, there;
And youthful voices there shall join
  With the angelic choir.
   CHORUS.

3 Our faithful teachers point the way,
  And guide our youthful steps aright,
To yonder world of endless day,
  Where Jesus is the light.
   CHORUS.

PRAYER.

Chant. The 67th Psalm:

"God be merciful unto us, and bless us; and cause his face to shine upon us." (*See Appendix.*)

Scripture Reading. Part of the 3d chapter of Galatians.

Singing. A selection. Solo, duet or quartette and chorus, or select piece by a class.

RECITATION.

By INFANT CLASS pupils:

First Voice. I'm a little pilgrim,
And a stranger here;
Though this earth is pleasant,
Sin is always near.

Second Voice. Jesus loves our little band,
He will lead us by the hand,
Lead us to that better land,
By-and-by.

Third Voice. Mine's a better country,
Where there is no sin,
Where the tones of sorrow
Never enter in.

Fourth Voice. But a little pilgrim
Must have garments clean,
Ere he'll wear the white robe,
And with Christ be seen.

Fifth Voice. Jesus, hear and save me;
Teach me to obey;
Holy Spirit guide me
In the heavenly way.

All. Jesus loves our little band,
He will lead us by the hand,
Lead us to that better land
By and by.

Singing. "The Better Land."—The Silver Spray, p. 91.

Shall I wear a crown of glory
In a better land?
Shall I tell the wondrous story
In the better land?

ABRAHAM.—THE CALL AND PROMISE.

Outline of Opening Remarks by the Superintendent. Abraham was born at Ur of the Chaldees (use a large map), between Nineveh and Nisibis—east and north from Palestine, beyond the Euphrates—year of the world 2009; after the deluge 350 years; was the son of Terah; his wife's name was Sarai; they were descendants of Shem. Ten generations from Adam to the deluge, and ten from the deluge to Abraham. His fathers were idolators—sun, moon, and stars were worshiped. The Bedouins, who inhabit the same country at the present time, doubtless resemble in many respects, the people of those ancient tribes. "The unchanged habits of the east render it, in this respect, a kind of *living Pompeii.*"

Terah, with his son *Abram* (for this was his name until God changed it to Abraham), emigrate to Mesopotamia, where Terah dies, and Abram pursues his course to the land of Canaan. God had directed him hither; here he received the promise of God that he should be the father of a great nation. We are now to study the lesson of this great promise.

Class A

Will repeat the Scripture concerning the call and promise to Abraham, as in Genesis, 12th chapter.

First Pupil. "Now the Lord had said unto Abram, Get thee out of thy country, and from thy kindred, and from thy father's house, unto a land that I will shew thee."—Gen. 12: 1.

Second Pupil. "And I will make of thee a great nation, and I will bless thee, and make thy name great; and thou shalt be a blessing."—Gen. 12: 2.

Third Pupil. "And I will bless them that bless thee, and curse him that curseth thee: and in thee shall all families of the earth be blessed."—Gen. 12: 3.

Fourth Pupil. "So Abram departed, as the Lord had spoken unto him; and Lot went with him; and Abram was seventy and five years old when he departed out of Haran."—Gen. 12: 4.

Fifth Pupil. "And Abram took Sarai his wife, and Lot his brother's son, and all their substance that they had gathered, and the souls that they had gotten in Haran; and they went forth to go into the land of Canaan; and into the land of Canaan they came."—Gen. 12: 5.

REMARKS.

* "Thus we view the little company of Abraham and his sister's son, nearly four thousand years ago, starting on a pilgrimage, 'as they went forth,' in obedience to God's call, 'to go to the *land of Canaan.*' All the substance that they had gathered is heaped high on the backs of their kneeling camels. Round about them, and underneath the towering forms of the camels, are their flocks.

"The chief is there amidst the stir of the movement, or may be seen at noonday resting within his tent. What a character was that chief in sacred history! With him the Old Testament history properly commences; that before being merely introductory to that grand movement which begins in Ur of the Chaldees, and ends with the final destruction of the Jewish polity and people."

What a long vista is opened in this beginning of that earthly journey to the earthly Canaan! This is the beginning of the nation whose history and country are prophetic of the heavenly Canaan. God had a revelation of salvation, of heaven and eternity, to make to a lost race whose intellects and hearts could not comprehend a single line of that revelation; and he set about giving to the world *object lessons* of heaven with the materials of earth. It was a great work to elevate the earthly conceptions of mortals to a contemplation of heavenly things. The whole line of history, from Abraham to Christ, is but a series of spiritual lessons, given in the language

* Stanley's History of the Jewish Church.

of earth. Surely the law has been the great schoolmaster to lead the world to Christ; but Christ came as the fulfillment of the law and the prophets, and took the world up from these primary lessons, and made the revelation plain by the higher method of his gospel.

Singing. "The Land of Promise."—The Silver Spray, p. 51.

1 Have you heard of the land of promise,
Far beyond the glowing sky?
There is rest for the faint and weary,
There shall pleasure never die.

CHORUS.—Come, oh come, and learn the story
Of the Christian's home in glory, etc.

2 Have ye heard of the heavenly Canaan,
Where the good shall part no more?
Join our band, we are marching onward,
Soon our journey will be o'er.

CHORUS.

3 Have ye heard of the holy city,
Beauteous realm of joy untold?
Would ye roam by the shining river?
Would ye tread the streets of gold?

CHORUS.

Supt. CLASS B will give some account of the journey of Abraham.

First Pupil. "And Abram passed through the land unto the place of Sichem, unto the plain of Moreh. And the Canaanite was then in the land."—Gen. 12: 6.

Second Pupil. "And the Lord appeared unto Abram, and said, Unto thy seed will I give this land: and there builded he an altar unto the Lord, who appeared unto him."—Gen. 12: 7.

Third Pupil. "And he removed from thence unto a mountain on the east of Bethel, and pitched his tent, having Bethel on the west, and Hai on the east; and there he builded an altar unto the Lord, and called upon the name of the Lord."—Gen. 12: 8.

Fourth Pupil. "And Abram journeyed, going on still toward the south."—Gen. 12: 9.

Fifth Pupil. "And there was a famine in the land: and Abram went down into Egypt to sojourn there; for the famine was grievous in the land."—Gen. 12: 10.

Supt. CLASS C will tell us of the return from Egypt of Abram and Lot.

First Pupil. "And Abram went up out of Egypt; he and his wife, and all that he had, and Lot with him, into the south." —Gen. 13: 1.

Second Pupil. "And Abram was very rich in cattle, in silver, and in gold."—Gen. 13: 2.

Third Pupil. "And he went on his journeys from the south even to Bethel, unto the place where his tent had been at the beginning, between Bethel and Hai."—Gen. 13: 3.

Fourth Pupil. "Unto the place of the altar, which he had made there at the first: and there Abram called on the name of the Lord."—Gen. 13: 4.

Fifth Pupil. "And Lot also, which went with Abram, had flocks, and herds, and tents."—Gen. 13: 5.

Sixth Pupil. "And there was a strife between the herdmen of Abram's cattle and the herdmen of Lot's cattle; and the Canaanite and the Perizzite dwelt then in the land."—Gen. 13: 7.

Seventh Pupil. "And Abram said unto Lot, let there be no strife, I pray thee, between me and thee, and between my herdmen and thy herdmen: for we be brethren."—Gen. 13: 8.

Eighth Pupil. "Is not the whole land before thee? separate thyself, I pray thee, from me: if thou wilt take the left hand, then I will go to the right; or if thou depart to the right hand, then I will go to the left."—Gen. 13: 9.

Supt. CLASS D.—The land promised to Abraham as an everlasting possession!

First Pupil. "And the Lord said unto Abram, after that Lot was separated from him, Lift up now thine eyes, and look from the place where thou art northward, and southward, and eastward, and westward: For all the land which thou seest, to thee will I give it, and to thy seed for ever."—Gen. 13: 14, 15.

Second Pupil. "And I will make thy seed as the dust of the earth: so that if a man can number the dust of the earth, then shall thy seed also be numbered."—Gen. 13: 16.

Third Pupil. "Arise, walk through the land in the length of it and in the breadth of it; for I will give it unto thee."—Gen. 13: 17.

Fourth Pupil. "Then Abram removed his tent, and came and dwelt in the plain of Mamre, which is in Hebron, and built there an altar unto the Lord."—Gen. 13: 18.

Supt. And the Lord encouraged Abraham!

Fifth Pupil. "After these things, the word of the Lord came unto Abram in a vision, saying, Fear not, Abram: I am thy shield, and thy exceeding great reward."—Gen. 15: 1.

Sixth Pupil. "And Abram said, Behold to me thou hast given no seed."—Gen. 15: 3.

Seventh Pupil. "And he brought him forth abroad, and said, Look, now, towards heaven, and tell the stars, if thou be able to number them. And he said unto him, So shall thy seed be."—Gen. 15: 4.

Eighth Pupil. "And he believed in the Lord; and he counted it to him for righteousness."—Gen. 15: 6.

Supt. CLASS E.—God's covenant with Abraham! Genesis, 17th chapter.

First Pupil. "And when Abram was ninety years old and nine, the Lord appeared to Abram, and said unto him, I am the Almighty God; walk before me, and be thou perfect."

Second Pupil. "And I will make my covenant between me and thee, and will multiply thee exceedingly."

Third Pupil. "And Abram fell on his face, and God talked with him, saying, As for me, behold, my covenant is with thee, and thou shalt be a father of many nations."

Supt. Abram's name is changed!

Fourth Pupil. "Neither shall thy name any more be called Abram, but thy name shall be Abraham; for a father of many nations have I made thee."

Fifth Pupil. "And I will establish my covenant between me and thee and thy seed after thee in their generations, for an everlasting covenant, to be a God unto thee and to thy seed after thee."

Sixth Pupil. "And I will give unto thee, and to thy seed after thee, the land wherein thou art a stranger, all the land of Canaan, for an everlasting possession; and I will be their God."

Singing. "Happy Voices," p. 53.

CANAAN.

Come, children, let us sweetly sing,
We're bound for the land of Canaan.

Supt. CLASS F.—Was the promise, "I will make of thee a great nation," fulfilled?

First Pupil. It was.

"And Solomon said unto God, Thou hast shewed great mercy unto David my father, and hast made me to reign in his stead. Now, O Lord God, let thy promise unto David my father be established: for thou hast made me king over a people like the dust of the earth in multitude."—2 Chron. 1: 8, 9.

Second Pupil. "And now, O Lord my God, thou hast made thy servant king instead of David my father: and I am but a little child: I know not how to go out or come in. And thy servant is in the midst of thy people which thou hast chosen, a great people, that cannot be numbered nor counted for multitude."—1 Kings 3: 7, 8.

Third Pupil. "Give therefore thy servant an understanding heart to judge thy people, that I may discern between good and bad: for who is able to judge this thy so great a people?"—1 Kings 3: 9.

Supt. CLASS G.—Was the promise, "In thee shall all the families of the earth be blessed," fulfilled?

First Pupil. "Know ye, therefore, that they which are of faith, the same are the children of Abraham."—Gal. 3: 7.

Second Pupil. "And the Scripture, foreseeing that God would justify the heathen through faith, preached before the gospel unto Abraham, saying, In thee shall all nations be blessed."—Gal. 3: 8.

Third Pupil. "So then they which be of faith are blessed with faithful Abraham."—Gal. 3: 9.

Fourth Pupil. "For verily he took not on him the nature of angels; but he took on him the seed of Abraham."— Heb. 2: 16.

Fifth Pupil. "Wherefore in all things it behooved him to be made like unto his brethren, that he might be a merciful and faithful high priest in things pertaining to God, to make reconciliation for the sins of the people."— Heb. 2: 17.

Supt. Who, then, are the true seed of Abraham?

A Teacher. "And if ye be Christ's, then are ye Abraham's seed, and heirs according to the promise."— Gal. 3: 29.

Another. "And I say unto you, that many shall come from the east and west, and shall sit down with Abraham, and Isaac, and Jacob, in the kingdom of heaven."— Matt. 8: 11.

Another. "For the promise, that he should be the heir of the world, was not to Abraham, or to his seed, through the law, but through the righteousness of faith."— Rom. 4: 13.

Supt. What of the spiritual fulfillment of these great promises to Abraham and to his seed?

A Teacher. "These all died in faith, not having received the promises, but having seen them afar off, and were persuaded of them, and embraced them, and confessed that they were strangers and pilgrims on the earth. For they that say such things declare plainly that they seek a country."— Heb. 11: 13, 14.

Another. "But now they desire a better country, that is, a heavenly: wherefore God is not ashamed to be called their God: for he hath prepared for them a city."— Heb. 11: 16.

Singing.

Glorious things of thee are spoken,
Zion, city of our God;

Or,

Beautiful Zion, built above.

FAMILIAR REMARKS

(Conversational) to the Children by the Superintendent or Pastor. We have named our exercise to-night "*A Lesson of Promise* (refer to the words written on the

board). Do we all know the meaning of this word *promise?* How many hands? Yes, your father and mother have made promises to you, and you knew what those promises meant. You trust in your parents because they never intentionally deceive you. That trust is your faith in them.

My dear children, the great God, who made this great and beautiful world, who made us, and by his wonderful power keeps us alive to-night, who never made a mistake or a false promise—our kind heavenly Father, has given us this blessed book, the Bible, full of his *exceedingly great and precious promises* to us. Do we believe them? Shall we take him at his word? Hands—yes, children, hold up your hands, if you mean it. This, then, is our faith in God. Let us now listen to some of God's promises, and as we do so, we will all try to look into our own hearts and see whether we can claim these precious promises to ourselves

PRECIOUS PROMISES.

A Teacher. These are the words of wisdom contained in Proverbs 8: 17: "I love them that love me; and those that seek me early shall find me."

Another. Christ said to his disciples, and he says to us, "If ye shall ask anything in my name, I will do it."

Another. "And all things, whatsoever ye shall ask in prayer, believing, ye shall receive."

Another. This is the Saviour's blessed invitation and promise to all sin-burdened souls: "Come unto me all ye that labor and are heavy laden, and I will give you rest. Take my yoke upon you, and learn of me; for I am meek and lowly in heart: and ye shall find rest unto your souls. For my yoke is easy, and my burden is light."

Another. Peter says: "The Lord is not slack concerning his promise, as some men count slackness; but is long-suffering to usward, not willing that any should perish, but that all should come to repentance."

Another. And Paul counsels his brethren: "Let us hold fast the profession of our faith without wavering; for he is faithful that promised."

Supt. "In my Father's house are many mansions: if it were not so, I would have told you. I go to prepare a place for you. And if I go and prepare a place for you, I will come again, and receive you unto myself; that where I am, there ye may be also."

Pastor. "Eye hath not seen, nor ear heard, neither have entered into the heart of man, the things which God hath prepared for them that love him."

Singing. The Doxology:

Praise God, from whom all blessings flow.

BENEDICTION.

III.

Abraham:

A LESSON OF FAITH.

"Looking unto Jesus, the author and finisher of our faith."—*Heb.* 12: 2.

"Above all, taking the shield of faith, wherewith ye shall be able to quench all the fiery darts of the wicked."—*Eph.* 6: 16.

EXERCISE.

Opening Song. "Blessed are they that believe." —The Silver Spray, p. 82 (or substitute).

Scripture Reading. Psalm 125. (*See Appendix.*)

PRAYER.

Chant. The 121st Psalm. (*See Appendix.*)

Supt. and School repeat in concert the "Apostles' Creed." (*See Appendix.*)

"I believe in God the Father Almighty, maker of heaven and earth;" etc.

Supt. will here announce the subject of the lesson, with the word FAITH on the board, and repeat the following:

"Abraham believed in the Lord; and he counted it to him for righteousness."—Gen. 15 : 6.

Ass't Supt. "But thou art holy, O thou that inhabitest the praises of Israel. Our fathers trusted in thee: they trusted, and thou didst deliver them. They cried unto thee, and were delivered: they trusted in thee, and were not confounded."—Ps. 22 : 3–5.

Pastor. "In thee, O Lord, do I put my trust; let me never be ashamed: deliver me in thy righteousness. Bow down thine ear to me; deliver me speedily: be thou my strong rock, for a house of defence to save me. For thou art my rock and my fortress: therefore for thy name's sake lead me, and guide me." —Ps. 31 : 1–3.

A Teacher—

On the truth I repose, nay, on thee, O my God,
For thou art the *Truth* to my soul;
No shadow, no phantom, no fiction of earth,
Shall rival thy gracious control.

Singing. "Confidence in Jesus."—Notes of Joy, p. 31.

I'll go by faith to Jesus,
To Jesus, to Jesus;
I'll tell my wants to Jesus,
My best and dearest friend.

CHORUS.—On Jesus, on Jesus,
I cast my every care,
And at the door of mercy
I'll seek his face in prayer.

Dialogue between a member of the Infant Class and one of the older scholars.

Ada. God is in heaven—can he hear
A feeble prayer like mine?
Lillie. Yes, little child, thou needst not fear:
He listeneth to thine.

A. God is in heaven—can he see
When I am doing wrong?
L. Yes, that he can; he looks at thee
All day and all night long.

A. God is in heaven—would he know
If I should tell a lie?
L. Yes, if thou saidst it very low,
He'd hear it in the sky.

A. God is in heaven—can I go
To thank him for his care?
L. Not yet; but love him here below
And thou shalt praise him there.

Opening Remarks to the Children by the Supt. The name of our lesson to-night is Faith. [Refer to word on the board.] What does it mean? [Not many hands.] Have I asked a hard question? Will some teacher please help us?

A Teacher. "Now faith is the substance of things hoped for, the evidence of things not seen."—Heb. 11 : 1.

Supt. That is what a very learned and inspired man once said about faith ; it is in the Bible, and it is true ; but some of us don't understand it yet.

Children, if I should promise to make each of you a present at the close of this lesson, do you believe I would do it? [Hands.] Yes, you believe this, because you know me; you have confidence in me, you take me at my word. Now think a moment, and then answer me : what is that knowledge and confidence, that belief in you, that I would fulfill my promise? We must have a name for it. [Hands.] Yes, it is your *faith* in me.

Now I will tell you of a great and good man who believed and trusted in God just as you would believe and trust in me. Our lesson to-night is about this good man. His name was Abraham.

* "Abraham and Sarah, his wife, lived in a tent in the land of Canaan. They had no little child. Abraham was a very old man, and Sarah was a very old woman. Abraham was almost a hundred years old, and Sarah was almost ninety.

"One night God said to Abraham, 'Come out of your tent and look up to the sky. What do you see?' The sky was full of stars, more than could be counted. Have you sometimes looked up into the sky on a clear starlight night? What a wonderful sight! How impossible it would be to count all those shining stars. And now I will tell you what the promise to Abraham was. And God said to Abraham, 'You shall have a great many grandchildren and great-grandchildren, and they shall have more children, till there are as many people as there are stars in the sky ; and they shall live in the land of Canaan, and the wicked people shall be turned out of it.'

"Now Abraham had not even one little child, yet he believed that God would do as he promised. He knew that God always speaks the truth and keeps his word."

And God did keep his promise to Abraham. The

* From "Line upon Line."

next year Sarah had a son. He was named Isaac. He was a good child, and God loved him. And God was pleased with Abraham for having so much faith in him.

Some one will give us a text about this.

A Teacher. And (Abraham) "staggered not at the promise of God through unbelief; but was strong in faith, giving glory to God: and being fully persuaded, that what he had promised, he was able also to perform. And therefore it was imputed to him for righteousness."— Rom. 4 : 20–22.

Supt. Soon our lesson will tell us about Isaac, and more about Abraham's faith, and how God tried his faith to see if it was true.

But perhaps some little child has thought, that, if we could only see God just as Abraham did, and hear him speak the promises, then it would be easier to have faith in God.

I think Jesus once said something to one of his disciples about that very thing. Will some one give us a text?

A Teacher. "And Thomas answered and said unto him, My Lord and my God. Jesus saith unto him, Thomas, because thou hast seen me, thou hast believed: blessed are they that have not seen, and yet have believed."—John 20 : 28, 29.

Supt. Shall we now have two or three of the Saviour's precious promises repeated from the Infant Class?

First Child. "Ask, and it shall be given you; seek, and ye shall find; knock, and it shall be opened unto you:"

Second Child. "For every one that asketh receiveth; and he that seeketh findeth; and to him that knocketh it shall be opened."

Third Child. "If ye then, being evil, know how to give good gifts unto your children, how much more shall your Father which is in heaven give good things to them that ask him?"

Supt. Let us all now look to God and ask him to strengthen our faith and give us the Holy Spirit.

BRIEF PRAYER BY THE SUPT.

Singing.

My faith looks up to thee,
Thou Lamb of Calvary.

Supt. We will now hear from the classes. CLASS A will tell us of Isaac, the child of promise. What was the blessing bestowed upon Sarah, the wife of Abraham?

First Pupil. "And God said unto Abraham, As for Sarai thy wife, thou shalt not call her name Sarai, but Sarah shall her name be. And I will bless her, and give thee a son also of her: yea, I will bless her, and she shall be a mother of nations; kings of people shall be of her."—Gen. 17: 15, 16.

Supt. How was Isaac connected with the covenant?

Second Pupil. "And God said, Sarah thy wife shall bear thee a son indeed; and thou shalt call his name Isaac: and I will establish my covenant with him for an everlasting covenant, and with his seed after him."—Gen. 17: 19.

Supt. Was God's promise to Sarah fulfilled?

Third Pupil. "And the Lord visited Sarah as he had said, and the Lord did unto Sarah as he had spoken. And Abraham called the name of his son that was born unto him, whom Sarah bare to him, Isaac."—Gen. 21: 1, 3.

Supt. Why was Isaac particularly dear to his father?

Fourth Pupil. Because he was the long-looked-for child of promise.

"But my covenant will I establish with Isaac, which Sarah shall bear unto thee at this set time in the next year."—Gen. 17: 21.

Supt. CLASS B will give us some account of the great trial to which Abraham was called, as recorded in Gen. 22.

First Pupil. "And it came to pass after these things, that God did tempt Abraham, and said unto him, Abraham: And and he said, Behold, here I am."

Second Pupil. "And he said, Take now thy son, thine only son Isaac, whom thou lovest, and get thee into the land of Moriah; and offer him there for a burnt offering upon one of the mountains which I will tell thee of."

Third Pupil. "And Abraham rose up early in the morning, and saddled his ass, and took two of his young men with him, and Isaac his son, and clave the wood for the burnt offering, and rose up, and went unto the place of which God had told him."

Fourth Pupil. "Then on the third day Abraham lifted up his eyes, and saw the place afar off."

Fifth Pupil. "And Abraham said unto his young men, Abide ye here with the ass; and I and the lad will go yonder and worship, and come again to you."

Sixth Pupil. "And Abraham took the wood of the burnt offering, and laid it upon Isaac his son; and he took the fire in his hand, and a knife; and they went both of them together."

Supt. CLASS C., what touching question did the lad put to his father, and what was the father's answer?

First Pupil. "And Isaac spake unto Abraham his father, and said, My father: and he said, Here am I, my son. And he said, Behold the fire and the wood: but where is the lamb for a burnt offering?"

Second Pupil. "And Abraham said, My son, God will provide himself a lamb for a burnt offering: so they went both of them together."

Supt. Children, I will write two words upon the board. These are the words:

JEHOVAH JIREH.

These are strange words to you, but you shall know the meaning of these words. I will write again. This is what the strange words mean:

GOD WILL PROVIDE.

Do you believe, my dear children, that God will provide for you in this world and in the world to come?

*"Abraham believed in God. His was the severest trial of faith the world ever knew. God had said to him, 'Take now thy son, thy only son, Isaac, whom thou lovest.' Every word went to his heart. 'Thy son,' the son of thy beloved Sarah, the son of the promise, the son by whom thou art expecting this land to be peopled, who is to transmit thy name and family to distant ages, and through whom all mankind are to be blest. 'Take him and get into the land of Moriah, and offer him there for a burnt offering.' What a blight to all his hopes, and what a shock to paternal feeling! Can it be that the son on whom God himself has caused such expectations to rest, must die? and not by disease incapable of being controlled, but in the midst of health? and that the father, whose heart during so many years has yearned over him with inexpressible tenderness, is himself to be the executioner? And this by command of the very Jehovah whose repeated assurances have caused such hopes to cluster about Isaac's life? Our faith is tested by the narrative; much more must Abraham's have been!"

Do we know that Abraham's faith was sufficient for this great trial?

Third Pupil of same class. "And they came to the place which God had told him of; and Abraham built an altar there, and laid the wood in order, and bound Isaac his son, and laid him on the altar upon the wood."

Fourth Pupil. "And Abraham stretched forth his hand, and took the knife to slay his son."

Supt. *Jehovah Jireh*—God will provide!

Fifth Pupil. "And the angel of the Lord called unto him out of heaven, and said, Abraham, Abraham: and he said, Here am I."

Sixth Pupil. "And he said, Lay not thine hand upon the lad, neither do thou anything unto him: for now I know that thou fearest God, seeing thou hast not withheld thy son, thine only son, from me."

* Sermons by Newman Hall.

Seventh Pupil. "And Abraham lifted up his eyes, and looked, and behold behind him a ram caught in a thicket by his horns: and Abraham went and took the ram and offered him up for a burnt offering in the stead of his son."

Eighth Pupil. "And Abraham called the name of that place Jehovah-jireh: as it is said to this day, In the mount of the Lord it shall be seen."

Supt. What promises were made to Abraham as a reward of his faith?

CLASS D.

First Pupil. "And the angel of the Lord called unto Abraham out of heaven the second time, and said, By myself have I sworn, saith the Lord, for because thou hast done this thing, and hast not withheld thy son, thine only son."—Gen. 22: 15, 16.

Second Pupil. "That in blessing I will bless thee, and in multiplying I will multiply thy seed as the stars of the heaven, and as the sand which is upon the seashore; and thy seed shall possess the gate of his enemies."—Gen. 22: 17.

Third Pupil. "And in thy seed shall all the nations of the earth be blessed; because thou hast obeyed my voice."—Gen. 22: 18.

Supt. What of the fulfillment of this great promise?

Fourth Pupil. "Know ye therefore that they which are of faith, the same are the children of Abraham. So then they which be of faith are blessed with faithful Abraham."—Gal. 3: 7, 9.

Fifth Pupil. "For ye are all the children of God by faith in Christ Jesus. For as many of you as have been baptized into Christ have put on Christ. There is neither Jew nor Greek, there is neither bond nor free, there is neither male nor female: for ye are all one in Christ Jesus."—Gal. 3: 26–28.

Sixth Pupil. "And if ye be Christ's, then are ye Abraham's seed, and heirs according to the promise."—Gal. 3: 29

Seventh Pupil. "For verily he took not on him the nature of angels; but he took on him the seed of Abraham."—Heb. 2: 16.

Supt. We will now hear from the members of a BIBLE CLASS.*

First Pupil. "Salvation cannot be achieved: it must be provided. For a work so great we cannot venture to look to any created being. But when there was 'no eye to pity and no hand to save,' God himself provided eternal redemption for us. Of this the sacrifice of Isaac presents an impressive type; or at least a most instructive illustration. May not Abraham himself have beheld the greater sacrifice under the figure of the less?"

Second Pupil. "Was it partly to this our Lord alluded when he said, 'Your father Abraham rejoiced to see my day: he saw it and was glad'?"

Third Pupil. "The 'land of Moriah' was the hill country, on one of the crests of which was afterward crucified the divine Seed of Isaac, in whom all the families of the earth are to be blessed. The region was the same; the sites of the sacrifices may have been identical."

Fourth Pupil. "Isaac, carrying the wood on which he was to be placed as the victim, brings before us him who went forth bending beneath the cross on which he was to suffer."

Fifth Pupil. "In the voluntary submission of Isaac we are reminded of him who said, 'No man taketh my life from me; I lay it down of myself.'"

Sixth Pupil. "In the love of Abraham for his only son, Isaac, how emphatically is set forth the love of God to us in the unspeakable gift of Christ!"

Seventh Pupil. "The voice from heaven, 'Now I know that thou fearest God, seeing thou hast not withheld thy son, thy only son, from me,' is a prelude to that other word, uttered by the Lord of angels himself: 'God so loved the world, that he gave his only begotten Son, that whosoever believeth in him should not perish, but have everlasting life!'"

Supt. or Pastor. "Divine justice leads us to the place of sacrifice where the law, dishonored by disobedience of its precepts, must be magnified by the exaction of its penalty. Bound to the altar with fetters which no mortal strength can burst, and at the point of death, we hear the voice from heaven,

* The recitations in this class are from "Sermons by Newman Hall, D. D."

'Behold the Lamb of God which taketh away the sin of the world.' We 'believe in the Lord Jesus Christ,' who says, 'Look unto me and be ye saved.' Our fetters fall. Then confessing our guilt, the prayer is heard, 'God be merciful to me a sinner.' There is now 'no condemnation for them who are in Christ Jesus.' In him we have eternal life. Surely, then, with Abraham we may adore the Lord our provider, and on the altar where Christ suffered for us we will inscribe — JEHOVAH JIREH!"

A Lady Teacher.

Though troubles assail, and dangers affright,
Though friends should all fail, and foes all unite,
Yet one thing secures us, whatever betide,—
The Scripture assures us the Lord will provide.

Another.

When life sinks apace, and death is in view,
The word of his grace shall comfort us through;
No fearing or doubting, with Christ on our side,
We hope to die shouting — the Lord will provide!

Closing Song. "Happy Voices," p. 218.

A crown of glory bright,
By faith I see.

IV.

Moses,

THE EGYPTIAN, THE EXILE, THE LEADER:

A LESSON OF GOD IN HISTORY.

"And there arose not a prophet since in Israel like unto Moses, whom the Lord knew face to face."—*Deut.* 34. 10.

"The eternal God is thy refuge, and underneath are the everlasting arms."—*Deut.* 33: 27.

EXERCISE.

Singing. The Doxology:

Praise God from whom all blessings flow.

PRAYER.

Superintendent—read. "And God spake unto Israel in the visions of the night, and said, Jacob, Jacob. And he said, Here am I. And he said, I am God, the God of thy father: fear not to go down into Egypt; for I will there make of thee a great nation. I will go down with thee into Egypt; and I will also surely bring thee up again: and Joseph shall put his hand upon thine eyes."—Gen. 46: 2-4.

"And Israel said unto Joseph, Behold, I die; but God shall be with you. and bring you again unto the land of your fathers." —Gen. 48: 21.

Singing. "Hail to the Brightness of Zion's Glad Morning." (2 verses.)

Assistant Superintendent. "And Pharaoh charged all his people, saying, Every son that is born ye shall cast into the river, and every daughter ye shall save alive."—Ex. 1: 22.

Pastor—read. Ex. 2: 1-10.

Asst. Supt. "By faith Moses, when he was come to years, refused to be called the son of Pharaoh's daughter; choosing rather to suffer affliction with the people of God, than to enjoy the pleasures of sin for a season; esteeming the reproach of Christ greater riches than the treasures in Egypt; for he had respect unto the recompense of the reward."—Heb. 11: 24-26.

Supt.—read. "And it came to pass in those days, when Moses was grown, that he went out unto his brethren, and looked on their burdens: and he spied an Egyptian smiting a

Hebrew, one of his brethren. And he looked this way and that way, and when he saw that there was no man, he slew the Egyptian and hid him in the sand. And when he went out the second day, behold, two men of the Hebrews strove together: and he said to him that did the wrong, Wherefore smitest thou thy fellow? And he said, Who made thee a prince and a judge over us? intendest thou to kill me, as thou killedst the Egyptian? And Moses feared, and said, Surely this thing is known. Now when Pharaoh heard this thing, he sought to slay Moses. But Moses fled from the face of Pharaoh, and dwelt in the land of Midian: and he sat down by a well."—Ex. 2: 11–15.

Asst. Supt. "And it came to pass in process of time, that the king of Egypt died: and the children of Israel sighed by reason of the bondage, and they cried, and their cry came up unto God by reason of the bondage. And God heard their groaning, and God remembered his covenant with Abraham, with Isaac, and with Jacob. And God looked upon the children of Israel, and God had respect unto them."—Ex. 2: 23–25.

Supt. "Now Moses kept the flock of Jethro, his father-in-law, the priest of Midian: and he led the flock to the backside of the desert, and came to the mountain of God, even to Horeb. And the angel of the Lord appeared unto him in a flame of fire out of the midst of a bush: and he looked, and behold the bush burned with fire, and the bush was not consumed."—Ex. 3: 1–2.

Pastor. "The rocky ground at once became 'holy,' and the shepherd's sandal was to be taken off no less than on the threshold of a palace, or a temple. The call or revelation was two-fold: 1. The declaration of the Sacred Name expresses the eternal self-existence of the One God. 2. The mission was given to Moses to deliver his people. The two signs are characteristic—the one of his past Egyptian life, the other of his active shepherd life. In the rush of leprosy into his hand is the link between him and his people, whom the Egyptians called a nation of lepers. In the transformation of his shepherd's staff is the glorification of the simple pastoral life, of which that staff was the symbol, unto the great career which lay before it. Moses was now eighty years old. Forty years of his life he had passed in the palace of Pharaoh, and forty years in meditation in the wilderness, but his work was now before him, and obeying the call he returned to Egypt."

RECITATION.

A Teacher.

I have done, at length, with dreaming; henceforth, O thou soul of mine,
Thou must take up sword and gauntlet, waging warfare most divine.
Life is struggle, combat, victory! Wherefore have I slumbered on,
With my forces all unmarshaled, with my weapons all undrawn?
Oh! how many a glorious record had the angels of me kept,
Had I done instead of doubted; had I warred instead of wept!
Yet, my soul, look not behind thee! thou hast work to do at last.
Let the brave toil of the present overarch the crumbled past.
Build thy great acts high and higher; build them on the conquered sod:
Where thy weakness first fell bleeding, and thy first prayer rose to God.

Singing.

On the mountain top appearing,
Lo! the sacred herald stands.

Supt. What was the success of Moses with Pharaoh?

CLASS A.

First Pupil. "And the Lord said unto Moses, Pharaoh shall not hearken unto you; that my wonders may be multiplied in the land of Egypt."—Ex. 11: 9.

Second Pupil. "And Moses and Aaron did all these wonders before Pharaoh: and the Lord hardened Pharaoh's heart, so that he would not let the children of Israel go out of his land."—Ex. 11: 10.

Third Pupil. "For I will pass through the land of Egypt this night, and will smite all the first-born in the land of Egypt, both man and beast; and against all the gods of Egypt I will execute judgment: I am the Lord."—Ex. 12: 12.

Fourth Pupil. "And Pharaoh rose up in the night, he and all his servants, and all the Egyptians; and there was a great cry in Egypt: for there was not a house where there was not one dead."—Ex. 12: 30.

Fifth Pupil. "And he called for Moses and Aaron by night, and said, Rise up, and get you forth from among my people, both ye and the children of Israel; and go, serve the Lord, as ye have said."—Ex. 12: 31.

Sixth Pupil. "And it came to pass the selfsame day, that the Lord did bring the children of Israel out of the land of Egypt by their armies."—Ex. 12: 51.

Seventh Pupil. "And the Lord went before them by day in a pillar of a cloud, to lead them the way; and by night in a pillar of fire, to give them light; to go by day and night."—Ex. 13: 21.

Eighth Pupil. "He took not away the pillar of the cloud by day, nor the pillar of fire by night, from before the people."—Ex. 13: 22.

RECITATION,

Or to be Sung as a Duet or Quartette.

LEAD THOU ME ON.

Send kindly light amid the encircling gloom,
And lead me on!
The night is dark, and I am far from home;
Lead thou me on!
Keep thou my feet; I do not ask to see
The distant scene; one step's enough for me.

I was not ever thus, nor prayed that thou
Should'st lead me on.
I loved to choose, and see my path; but now
Lead thou me on!
I loved days dazzling; and spite of fears
Pride ruled my will; remember not past years!

So long thy power hath blessed me; surely still
'Twill lead me on
Through dreary doubt, through pain and sorrow, till
The night is gone;
And with the morn those angel faces smile
Which I have loved long since, and lost awhile.

J. H. Newman.

RECITATION.

INFANT CLASS.

First Pupil.

We have heard of the dear little baby,
  In the bulrushes hid away;
We have heard of the beauteous lady,
  Who walked by the stream that day.

Second Pupil.

And how Moses lived in the palace,
  And in knowledge and stature grew,
And how for the sake of his kindred,
  He the cruel Egyptian slew.

Third Pupil.

We have heard of the bush on Mount Horeb,
  How God spake through the fiery flame,
And bade him deliver his people,
  Alone in Jehovah's name.

Fourth Pupil.

But what is the lesson, dear teacher,
  Which a child may learn from his life?
Canst tell me what we may gather
  From this tale of toil and strife?

Teacher.

The lesson, dear children, which God would teach,
  Is to follow wherever he calls:
When he says to us, Soul, thy work is here,
We shall labor there — seek no other sphere —
  Though in desert, or palace walls.

God knoweth our strength, and our weakness too,
  And our needs he will supply;
If we do our part, and then trust to him,
Although the way be dark and dim,
  It will brighten by and by.

Supt. What is related of the children of Israel in the third month of their departure from Egypt?

CLASS B.

First Pupil. "In the third month, when the children of Israel were gone forth out of the land of Egypt, the same day came they into the wilderness of Sinai."—Ex. 19: 1.

Second Pupil. "And it came to pass, on the third day in the morning, that there were thunders and lightnings, and a thick cloud upon the mount, and the voice of the trumpet exceeding loud; so that all the people that was in the camp trembled."—Ex. 19: 16.

Third Pupil. "And the Lord came down upon mount Sinai, on the top of the mount: and the Lord called Moses up to the top of the mount; and Moses went up."—Ex. 19: 20.

Fourth Pupil. "And mount Sinai was altogether on a smoke, because the Lord descended upon it in fire: and the smoke thereof ascended as the smoke of a furnace, and the whole mount quaked greatly."—Ex. 19: 18.

Fifth Pupil. "And when the voice of the trumpet sounded long, and waxed louder and louder, Moses spake, and God answered him by a voice."—Ex. 19: 19.

Sixth Pupil. "So Moses went down unto the people, and spake unto them."—Ex. 19: 25.

Supt. "And God spake all these words, saying, I am the Lord thy God, which have brought thee out of Egypt, out of the house of bondage. Thou shalt have no other gods before me."

Response Chanted by Choir. Lord have mercy upon us, and incline our hearts to keep this law.

Supt. "Thou shalt not make unto thee any graven image, or any likeness of anything that is in heaven above, or that is in the earth beneath, or that is in the water under the earth: Thou shalt not bow down thyself to them, nor serve them; for I the Lord thy God am a jealous God, visiting the iniquity of the fathers upon the children unto the third and fourth generation of them that hate me; and showing mercy unto thousands of them that love me and keep my commandments."

Response. Lord have mercy upon us, and incline our hearts to keep this law.

Supt. "Thou shalt not take the name of the Lord thy God in vain: for the Lord will not hold him guiltless that taketh his name in vain."

Response. Lord have mercy upon us, and incline our hearts to keep this law.

Supt. "Remember the sabbath day, to keep it holy. Six days shalt thou labor, and do all thy work: But the seventh day is the sabbath of the Lord thy God: in it thou shalt not do any work, thou, nor thy son, nor thy daughter, thy man-servant, nor thy maid-servant, nor thy cattle, nor thy stranger that is within thy gates: for in six days the Lord made heaven and earth, the sea, and all that in them is, and rested the seventh day: wherefore the Lord blessed the sabbath day and hallowed it."

Response. Lord have mercy upon us, and incline our hearts to keep this law.

Supt. "Honor thy father and thy mother: that thy days may be long upon the land which the Lord thy God giveth thee."

Response. Lord have mercy upon us, and incline our hearts to keep this law.

Supt. "Thou shalt not kill."

Response. Lord have mercy upon us, and incline our hearts to keep this law.

Supt. "Thou shalt not commit adultery."

Response. Lord have mercy upon us, and incline our hearts to keep this law.

Supt. "Thou shalt not steal."

Response. Lord have mercy upon us, and incline our hearts to keep this law.

Supt. "Thou shalt not bear false witness against thy neighbor."

Response. Lord have mercy upon us, and incline our hearts to keep this law.

Supt. "Thou shalt not covet thy neighbor's house, thou shalt not covet thy neighbor's wife, nor his man-servant, nor his maid-servant, nor his ox, nor his ass, nor any thing that is thy neighbor's."

Response. Lord have mercy upon us, and write all these thy laws in our hearts, we beseech thee.

Supt. Did the children of Israel obey God?

Class C.

First Pupil. "And the Lord said unto Moses, How long will this people provoke me? and how long will it be ere they believe me, for all the signs which I have shewed among them?"—Num. 14: 11.

Second Pupil. "I will smite them with the pestilence, and disinherit them, and will make of thee a greater nation and mightier than they."—Num. 14: 12.

Third Pupil. "And Moses said unto the Lord, Pardon, I beseech thee, the iniquity of this people according unto the greatness of thy mercy. and as thou hast forgiven this people, from Egypt even until now."—Num. 14: 13. 19.

Fourth Pupil. "And the Lord said, I have pardoned according to thy word: but as truly as I live, all the earth shall be filled with the glory of the Lord."—Num. 14: 20, 21.

Fifth Pupil. "Because all those men which have seen my glory, and my miracles, which I did in Egypt and in the wilderness, and have tempted me now these ten times, and have not hearkened to my voice,"—Num. 14: 22.

Sixth Pupil. "Surely they shall not see the land which I sware unto their fathers, neither shall any of them that provoked me see it."—Num. 14: 23.

Supt. Was this judgment executed?

CLASS D.

First Pupil. "These are they that were numbered by Moses and Eleazar the priest, who numbered the children of Israel in the plains of Moab by Jordan near Jericho."—Num. 26: 63.

Second Pupil. "But among these there was not a man of them whom Moses and Aaron the priest numbered, when they numbered the children of Israel in the wilderness of Sinai."—Num. 26: 64.

Third Pupil. "For the Lord had said of them, They shall surely die in the wilderness. And there was not left a man of them, save Caleb the son of Jephunneh, and Joshua the son of Nun."—Num. 26: 65.

Supt. What concerning the death of Moses?

CLASS E.

First Pupil. "And the Lord spake unto Moses that selfsame day, saying, Get thee up into this mountain Abarim, unto mount Nebo, which is in the land of Moab, that is over against

Jericho; and behold the land of Canaan, which I give unto the children of Israel for a possession,"—Deut. 32: 48, 49.

Second Pupil. "And die in the mount whither thou goest up, and be gathered unto thy people; as Aaron thy brother died in mount Hor, and was gathered unto his people;"—Deut. 32: 50.

Third Pupil. "Because ye trespassed against me among the children of Israel at the waters of Meribah-Kadesh, in the wilderness of Zin; because ye sanctified me not in the midst of the children of Israel."—Deut. 32: 51.

Fourth Pupil. "Yet thou shalt see the land before thee; but thou shalt not go thither unto the land which I give the children of Israel."—Deut. 32: 52.

Fifth Pupil. "And Moses went up from the plains of Moab unto the mountain of Nebo, to the top of Pisgah, that is over against Jericho: and the Lord shewed him all the land of Gilead, unto Dan."—Deut. 34: 1.

Sixth Pupil. "And the Lord said unto him, This is the land which I sware unto Abraham, unto Isaac, and unto Jacob, saying, I will give it unto thy seed: I have caused thee to see it with thine eyes, but thou shalt not go over thither."—Deut. 34: 4.

Singing. "There is a land of pure delight."—Happy Voices, p. 212.

Teacher. "So Moses the servant of the Lord died there in the land of Moab, according to the word of the Lord."—Deut. 34: 5.

RECITATION.

THE BURIAL OF MOSES.

"And he buried him in a valley in the land of Moab, over against Beth-Peor; but no man knoweth of his sepulchre unto this day."—Deut. 34: 6.

1 By Nebo's lonely mountain,
  On this side Jordan's wave,
In a vale in the land of Moab,
  There lies a lonely grave.
And no man knows that sepulchre,
  And no man saw it e'er,
For the angels of God upturned the sod,
  And laid the dead man there.

2 That was the grandest funeral
That ever passed on earth;
But no man heard the trampling,
Or saw the train go forth —
Noiselessly, as the daylight
Comes back when night is done,
And the crimson streak on ocean's cheek
Grows into the great sun.

3 Noiselessly, as the spring-time
Her crown of verdure weaves,
And all the trees on all the hills
Open their thousand leaves,
So, without sound of music,
Or voice of them that wept,
Silently, down from mountain's crown
The great procession swept.

4 Perchance the bald old eagle,
On gray Beth-Peor's height,
Out of his lonely eyrie,
Looked on the wondrous sight.
Perchance the lion, stalking,
Still shuns that hallowed spot;
For beast and bird have seen and heard
That which man knoweth not.

5 But when the warrior dieth,
His comrades in the war,
With arms reversed, and muffled drum,
Follow his funeral car;
They show the banners taken;
They tell his battles won;
And after him lead his masterless steed,
While peals the minute-gun.

6 Amid the noblest of the land,
We lay the sage to rest,
And give the bard an honored place,
With costly marble drest,
In the great minster transept,
Where lights like glories fall,
And the organ rings and the sweet choir sings
Along the blazoned wall.

7 This was the truest warrior
  That ever buckled sword;
This the most gifted poet
  That ever breathed a word;
And never earth's philosopher
  Traced, with his golden pen,
On the deathless page, truths half so sage
  As he wrote down for men.

8 And had he not high honor—
  The hill-side for a pall,
To lie in state, while angels wait,
  With stars for tapers tall,
And the dark rock-pines, like tossing plumes,
  Over his bier to wave,
And God's own hand, in that lonely land,
  To lay him in the grave?

9 In that strange grave without a name,
  Whence his uncoffined clay
Shall break again, O wondrous thought!
  Before the judgment day,
And stand, with glory wrapped around,
  On the hills he never trod,
And speak of the strife that won our life,
  With th' incarnate Son of God.

10 O lonely grave in Moab's land!
  O dark Beth-Peor's hill!
Speak to these curious hearts of ours,
  And teach them to be still.
God hath his mysteries of grace,
  Ways that we cannot tell;
He hides them deep, like the hidden sleep
  Of him he loved so well.

Singing. "Pisgah's Mountains."—Fresh Laurels, p. 78.

1 Joyful, away to Pisgah's mountain,
  Borne on the wings of faith, we soar,
Sweetly we hear the echo ringing,
  Happy voices on the other shore.
Hark! they sing, in the bright vales of Eden,
  Songs of praise to the Lamb that was slain;
Round his throne with the martyrs they gather,
  There united forever to reign.

2 Christians, behold the hill of Zion,
See where our purest treasure lies.
Work for the Lord whate'er our trials;
Oh be faithful, we shall win the prize.
Crowned with light in a mansion of beauty,
We shall dwell with the pure and the blest;
We shall sing with the faithful in glory,
Where the weary forever shall rest.

3 We're pressing on with eager longing,
Pressing toward the swelling tide;
Jesus will bear us safely over,
We shall anchor on the other side.
Saved by grace, to his kingdom exalted,
When the billows of Jordan are passed,
We shall sing with the friends we have cherished,
Glory, glory, we're home, home at last.

V.

Isaiah:

A LESSON OF CHRIST IN PROPHECY.

"To him give all the prophets witness, that through his name, whosoever believeth in him, shall receive remission of sins."—*Acts* 10: 43.

"How beautiful upon the mountains are the feet of him that bringeth good tidings, that publisheth peace; that bringeth good tidings of good, that publisheth salvation; that saith unto Zion, thy God reigneth!"—*Isaiah* 52: 7.

EXERCISE.

Opening Song. "Olivet."

My faith looks up to thee,
Thou Lamb of Calvary,
Saviour divine.

Scripture Reading. The 53d chapter of Isaiah.

PRAYER

That this inspired testimony of the prophet may seal conviction in every heart, so that our faith in Christ may never waver.

Two boys recite:

1 Watchman, tell us of the night,
What its signs of promise are.

2 Traveler, o'er yon mountain's height,
See that glory-beaming star!

1 Watchman, does its beauteous ray
Aught of hope or joy foretell?

2 Traveler, yes; it brings the day,
Promised day of Israel.

1 Watchman, tell us of the night;
Higher yet that star ascends.

2 Traveler, blessedness and light,
Peace and truth its course portends.

1 Watchman, will its beams alone
Gild the spot that gave them birth?

2 Traveler, ages are its own;
See! it bursts o'er all the earth!

1 Watchman, tell us of the night,
For the morning seems to dawn.

2 Traveler, darkness takes its flight,
Doubt and terror are withdrawn.

1 Watchman, let thy wanderings cease;
Hie thee to thy quiet home.

2 Traveler, lo, the Prince of Peace,
Lo, the Son of God is come!

Singing. "Zion."

1 On the mountain's top appearing,
Lo, the sacred herald stands,
Welcome news to Zion bearing,
Zion long in hostile lands.
Mourning captive,
God himself will loose thy bands.

2 God, thy God, will now restore thee;
He himself appears thy friend:
All thy foes shall flee before thee;
Here their boasts and triumphs end;
Great deliverance
Zion's king vouchsafes to send.

Superintendent. We will to-night repeat some of the wonderful prophecies uttered by Isaiah hundreds of years before their fulfillment. Who will tell me how he was thus enabled to look into the future?

CLASS A.

First Pupil. "And he said, Hear now my words: If there be a prophet among you, I the Lord will make myself known unto him in a vision, and will speak unto him in a dream."—Num. 12: 6.

Second Pupil. "Come ye near unto me, hear ye this; I have not spoken in secret from the beginning; from the time that it was, there am I: and now the Lord God, and his Spirit, hath sent me."—Is. 48: 16.

Third Pupil. "The Lord God hath given me the tongue of the learned, that I should know how to speak a word in season to him that is weary: he wakeneth morning by morning, he wakeneth mine ear to hear as the learned."—Is. 50: 4.

Fourth Pupil. "And he said unto me, Son of man, stand upon thy feet, and I will speak unto thee. And the spirit entered into me when he spake unto me, and set me upon my feet, that I heard him that spake unto me."—Ezek. 2: 1, 2.

Fifth Pupil. "Surely the Lord God will do nothing, but he revealeth his secret unto his servants the prophets."—Amos 3: 7.

Sixth Pupil. "God, who at sundry times and in divers manners spake in time past unto the fathers by the prophets."—Heb. 1: 1.

Supt. How did the Jews divide the books of the Old Testament?

BIBLE CLASS.

First Pupil. Into the Law, the Prophets, and the Holy Writings.

Supt. What division is comprehended in the Prophets?

Second Pupil. The books of Joshua, Judges, 1 and 2 Samuel, 1 and 2 Kings, which were called "the former prophets," and Isaiah, Jeremiah, Ezekiel, and the books from Hosea to Malachi, which were called "the latter prophets."

Supt. What rank have Isaiah's prophecies held?

Third Pupil. They have been regarded as worthy of the principal place among the Jewish writings.

Supt. At what time in the world's history did he prophesy?

Fourth Pupil. From about 754 to 707 B. C.

Supt. Under what kings?

Fifth Pupil. "The vision of Isaiah the son of Amoz, which he saw concerning Judah and Jerusalem in the days of Uzziah, Jotham, Ahaz, and Hezekiah, kings of Judah."—Is. 1: 1.

Supt. What do we know of him under each of these kings?

Sixth Pupil. * "The first verse of the 6th chapter tells us, that he had a vision of Jehovah in the year in which Uzziah died. He occupied the prophetic office under Jotham sixteen years, during which time there is no express mention made of his uttering any prophecies; under Ahaz sixteen years, during whose ungodly reign he came forth boldly as the reprover of sin, but by whom his counsels and warnings were disregarded; under Hezekiah fourteen years, in whose reign he was treated with respect, and had an important part in directing the public counsels. How long he lived in Manasseh's time is not known; but the tradition is, that he was put to death by him by being sawn asunder."

Supt. Where did he reside?

Seventh Pupil. Probably in Jerusalem.

Supt. In what estimation is he held as a writer?

Eighth Pupil. He is regarded as the most sublime of all writers, even when his writings are considered as mere human compositions.

Supt. What is the natural division in the book of Isaiah?

Ninth Pupil. It is divided into two parts, the first of which closes with the 39th chapter, and the latter embraces the remainder of the book. The latter portion is almost an unbroken vision relating to far-distant events—the deliverance of the Jews from the bondage in Babylon, and the higher deliverance of the world under the Messiah. The former part embraces a collection of independent writings, designed to produce an immediate effect on the morals, the piety, the faith and the welfare of the nation.

Supt. Isaiah is sometimes called "the fifth Evangelist," or "the Evangelical Prophet." He is quoted eleven times by the New Testament writers in his exact words, twenty times in nearly the same words, and there is still a much larger number of quotations which agree in sense but not in words. Although he lived so many hundreds of years before the Evangelists who witnessed the events which they

* Barnes.

have recorded of the life, sufferings, and death of our Saviour, we find that he has described them almost as minutely as they have, and has the plan of salvation more clearly before his eyes than it was before their's until after Christ had ascended, and the Holy Spirit had brought to their remembrance all things that he had said unto them.

Will some member of CLASS B tell me if he prophesied correctly concerning the genealogy of the man Christ Jesus.

CLASS B.

First Pupil. He did, and this is the prophecy: "And in that day there shall be a root of Jesse, which shall stand for an ensign of the people; to it shall the Gentiles seek: and his rest shall be glorious."—Is. 11: 10.

Supt. What did he prophesy about his preaching?

Second Pupil. "The spirit of the Lord God is upon me; because the Lord hath anointed me to preach good tidings unto the meek; he hath sent me to bind up the broken-hearted, to proclaim liberty to the captives, and the opening of the prison to them that are bound."—Is. 61: 1.

RECITATION.

1 Upon the well by Sychar's gate,
At burning noon the Saviour sate,
Athirst and hungry from the way
His feet had trod since early day.
The twelve had gone to seek for food,
And left him in his solitude.

2 They come, and spread before him there,
With faithful haste, the pilgrim's fare,
And gently bid him, "Master, eat!"
But God had sent him better meat,
And there is on his lowly brow
Nor weariness nor faintness now;

3 For while they sought the market-place,
His words had won a soul to grace;
And when he set that sinner free
From bonds of guilt and infamy,
His heart grew strong with joy divine,
More than the strength of bread and wine.

4 So, Christian, when thy faith grows faint
Amidst the toils that throng the saint,
Ask God, that thou may'st peace impart
Unto some other human heart;
And thou thy Master's joy shalt share,
E'en while his cross thy shoulders bear.

G. W. Bethune.

Supt. Did Isaiah know of the miracles that Christ so many years afterwards was to perform?

Third Pupil. "Then the eyes of the blind shall be opened, and the ears of the deaf shall be unstopped. Then shall the lame man leap as a hart, and the tongue of the dumb sing; for in the wilderness shall waters break out, and streams in the desert."—Is. 35: 5, 6.

Supt. Did he tell of his sinless life?

Fourth Pupil. "He had done no violence, neither was any deceit in his mouth."—Is. 53: 9.

Supt. What about his silence at the trial?

Fifth Pupil. "He was oppressed and he was afflicted, yet he opened not his mouth; he is brought as a lamb to the slaughter, and as a sheep before her shearers is dumb, so he openeth not his mouth."—Is. 53: 7.

Supt. Did he foresee the scourging and contempt?

Sixth Pupil. "He is despised and rejected of men; a man of sorrows, and acquainted with grief; and we hid as it were our faces from him; he was despised, and we esteemed him not."—Is. 53: 3.

Supt. What did he say of his companions in crucifixion, and his intercession?

Seventh Pupil. "Therefore will I divide him a portion with the great, and he shall divide the spoil with the strong; because he hath poured out his soul unto death: and he was numbered with the transgressors; and he bare the sin of many, and made intercession for the transgressors."—Is. 53: 12.

Supt. What of the sacrifice and propitiation?

Eighth Pupil. "Surely he hath borne our griefs, and carried our sorrows; yet we did esteem him stricken, smitten of God, and afflicted. But he was wounded for our transgressions, he was bruised for our iniquities: the chastisement of our peace was upon him; and with his stripes we are healed."—Is. 53: 4, 5.

Singing. From "Fresh Laurels," p. 35.

1 Light and comfort of my soul,
When the billows o'er me roll;
Thou dost bid me in thy word,
Cast my burden on the Lord.
Jesus, Saviour once betrayed,
Sacrifice for sinners made;
Wretched, lost, to thee I fly,
Save, oh save me, or I die.

2 Lord, my soul in tears would mourn,
All the anguish thou hast borne;
In the garden I would be,
Lonely watcher still with thee.
Thou hast suffered, thou hast bled.
Thorns have pierced thy sacred head;
Jesus, while I cling to thee,
Let thy sorrow plead for me.

3 Mocked and scourged—condemned to die,
On the cross extended high;
Tenant of the lonely tomb,
Mighty conqueror o'er its gloom,
Crowned victorious God of love,
To thy Father's home above,
Grant my soul a place at last,
When the storms of life are past.

Supt. What did the prophet say concerning Christ's divinity and power?

CLASS C.

First Pupil. "For unto us a child is born, unto us a son is given: and the government shall be upon his shoulder; and his name shall be called Wonderful, Counsellor, The Mighty God, The Everlasting Father, The Prince of Peace."—Is. 9: 6.

Supt. Christ said, "I am the Good Shepherd." Did Isaiah apply to him this name?

Second Pupil. "He shall feed his flock like a shepherd: he shall gather the lambs with his arm, and carry them in his bosom."—Is. 40: 11.

Supt. Where does he speak of him as a corner-stone?

Third Pupil. In the 28th chapter, 16th verse: "Therefore thus saith the Lord God, Behold, I lay in Zion for a foundation a stone, a tried stone, a precious corner-stone, a sure foundation: he that believeth shall not make haste."

Supt. How does he encourage us in the 1st chapter, 18th verse?

Fourth Pupil. "Come, now, and let us reason together, saith the Lord: though your sins be as scarlet, they shall be as white as snow: though they be red like crimson, they shall be as wool."

Supt. How does he speak of our Lord's compassion?

Fifth Pupil. "A bruised reed shall he not break, and the smoking flax shall he not quench."—Is. 42: 3.

Supt. In what words does he tell us of the freeness of salvation?

Sixth Pupil. "Ho, every one that thirsteth, come ye to the waters, and he that hath no money; come ye, buy and eat; yea, come, buy wine and milk without money and without price."—Is. 55: 1.

Singing. "The Water of Life."—Fresh Laurels, p. 50.

Supt. To whose righteousness are we told to look?

Class D.

First Pupil. "I bring near my righteousness; it shall not be far off, and my salvation shall not tarry: and I will place salvation in Zion for Israel my glory."—Is. 46: 13.

Supt. What other promises does he bring to us?

Second Pupil. "I, even I, am he that blotteth out thy transgressions for mine own sake, and will not remember thy sins."—Is. 43: 25.

Third Pupil. "For the mountains shall depart, and the hills be removed; but my kindness shall not depart from thee, neither shall the covenant of my peace be removed, saith the Lord that hath mercy on thee."—Is. 54: 10.

Fourth Pupil. "Look unto me, and be ye saved, all the ends of the earth: for I am God, and there is none else."—Is. 45: 22.

RECITATION.

1 I lay my sins on Jesus,
The spotless Lamb of God;
He bears them all, and frees us
From the accursed load.

2 I lay my wants on Jesus,
All fullness dwells in him;
He healeth my diseases,
He doth my soul redeem.

3 I lay my griefs on Jesus,
My burdens and my cares;
He from them all releases,
He all my sorrows shares.

4 I long to be like Jesus,
Meek, loving, lowly, mild;
I long to be like Jesus,
The Father's holy child.

5 I long to be with Jesus,
Amid the heavenly throng,
To sing with saints his praises,
To learn the angels' song.

Supt. Where does he speak of Christ as our hiding-place?

CLASS E.

First Pupil. "And a man shall be as a hiding-place from the wind, and a covert from the tempest; as rivers of water in a dry place, as the shadow of a great rock in a weary land."—Is. 32: 2.

Singing.

Rock of ages, cleft for me,
Let me hide myself in thee.

Supt. Does he teach us to look for a full understanding of God's ways?

Second Pupil. "For my thoughts are not your thoughts, neither are your ways my ways, saith the Lord."—Is. 55: 8.

Supt. How are we assured of God's everlasting remembrance?

Third Pupil. "Behold, I have graven thee upon the palms of my hands; thy walls are continually before me."—Is. 49: 16.

Supt. How does he prompt us to a full assurance of faith?

Fourth Pupil. "Behold, God is my salvation; I will trust, and not be afraid: for the Lord Jehovah is my strength and my song; he also is become my salvation. Therefore with joy shall ye draw water out of the wells of salvation."—Is. 12: 2, 3.

Supt. How are we assured of the power of prayer?

Fifth Pupil. "Before they call, I will answer; and while they are yet speaking, I will hear."—Is. 65: 24.

RECITATION.

THE CHILD'S PRAYER.

1 Into her chamber went
A little girl one day;
And by a chair she knelt,
And thus began to pray:
"Jesus, my eyes I close,
Thy form I cannot see;

If thou art near me, Lord,
I pray thee speak to me."
A still small voice
She heard within her soul:
"What is it child? I hear;
I hear thee: tell me all."

2 "I pray thee, Lord," she said,
"That thou wilt condescend
To tarry in my heart,
And ever be my friend.
The path of life is dark—
I would not go astray;
Oh! let me have thy hand
To lead me in the way."
"Fear not, I will not leave
Thee, poor child, alone;"
And then she *thought* she felt
A soft hand press her own.

3 "They tell me, Lord, that all
The living pass away;
The aged *soon* must die,
And even children may:
Oh! let my parents live
Till I a woman grow,
For if *they* die, what can
A little orphan do?"
"Fear not, my child,
Whatever ills may come;
I'll not forsake thee e'er,
Until I bring thee home."

4 The little prayer was said,
And from her chamber now
She passed forth with the light
Of heaven upon her brow.
"Mother, I've seen the Lord—
His hand in mine I felt,
And oh! I heard him say,
As by my chair I knelt,
'Fear not, my child,
Whatever ills may come;
I'll not forsake thee e'er
Until I bring thee home.'"

Supt. How does this Gospel Prophet represent to us Christ's sympathy in our sorrows?

Sixth Pupil. "In all their affliction he was afflicted."—Is. 63: 9.

Supt. What promise for the church?

Seventh Pupil. "For thy Maker is thine husband; The Lord of Hosts is his name: and thy Redeemer the Holy One of Israel; The God of the Whole Earth shall he be called."—Is. 54: 5.

Singing.

1 I love thy church, O God,
Her walls before thee stand,
Dear as the apple of thine eye,
And graven on thy hand.

2 Sure as thy truth shall last,
To Zion shall be given
The brightest glories earth can yield,
And brighter bliss of heaven.

A few words from the Pastor.

Chant a portion of the prophecy of Zacharias (*see Appendix*), and close with the Doxology.

VI.

The Mountains of the Bible:

A LESSON CONCERNING THE EARTHLY SCENES OF GOD'S GLORY.

"As the mountains are round about Jerusalem, so the Lord is round about his people from henceforth even forever."—*Ps.* 125: 2.

"And I looked, and lo, a Lamb stood on Mount Zion, and with him a hundred forty and four thousand, having his Father's name written in their foreheads."—*Rev.* 14: 1.

EXERCISE.

Opening Song. "The Mount of Blessing."—Notes of Joy, p. 66.

We are climbing the mount of blessing,
We are seeking a city most fair.

Supt. and School. The Lord's Prayer.

Supt. reads the 90th or the 125th Psalm.

PRAYER.

Song. "The Shining Hills of Glory."—Fresh Laurels, p. 117.

RECITATION.

"Beautiful things above." (*See Appendix.*)

Song. "Beautiful Land."—Happy Voices, p. 193.

Supt. announces the subject of the exercise, "The Mountains of the Bible," and reads or repeats—

"The word that Isaiah the son of Amoz saw concerning Judah and Jerusalem. And it shall come to pass in the last days, that the mountain of the Lord's house shall be established in the top of the mountains, and shall be exalted above the hills; and all nations shall flow unto it. And many people shall go and say, Come ye, and let us go up to the mountain of the Lord, to the house of the God of Jacob; and he will teach us of his ways, and we will walk in his paths; for out of Zion shall go forth the law, and the word of the Lord from Jerusalem."—Isaiah 2: 1–3.

* "Mountains are among the most sublime and impressive of the Creator's works on earth, and form the noblest and most enduring monuments of great events. Most of the mountains of Scripture thus stand as witnesses for God — every view of their lofty summits, and every recurrence to them in thought reminding us of the sacred facts and truths connected with them. They are the silent, yet the most eloquent historians of heaven and earth."

MOUNT ARARAT.

Supt. The history of the deluge gives our first sacred mountain. On what mountain did the ark rest after the deluge?

First Pupil. "The ark rested, in the seventh month, on the seventeenth day of the month, upon the mountains of Ararat." — Gen. 8 : 4.

Supt. Where is Mount Ararat?

Bible Class Pupil, pointing locality on the map. "Mount Ararat is in Armenia, in western Asia, between the Caspian and the Black Seas. The first named summit in human history, it emerges from the flood, and lifts its head over the water to look down on all coming generations to the end of time. Baptized by the flood, consecrated by the altar, illumined by the first fresh rainbow, Mount Ararat stands a *sacred mountain* on the earth."

NOTE.— In the performance of this exercise, a large map of Palestine and one showing Armenia should be used, and a class of young ladies, to whom the "Map Lessons" have been assigned, should be so seated, that, when their respective parts are called, each may be able to approach the map and give the location with the pointer as she recites the part, in answer to the questions.

MOUNT MORIAH.

Supt. What mountain was the scene of Abraham's trial of faith?

Third Pupil. Mount Moriah: "Take now thy son, thine only son, Isaac, whom thou lovest, and get thee into the land of Moriah; and offer him there for a burnt-offering, upon one of the mountains which I will tell thee of."— Gen. 22 : 2.

* The descriptive language of the "Map Lessons" in this exercise is taken largely from "Sacred Mountains," by J. T. Headley.

Bible Class Pupil. (Map Lesson.) Mount Moriah, according to Jewish tradition, is one of the hills on which Jerusalem was built. It is separated from the Mount of Olives by the valley of Jehoshaphat. It is 2,000 feet above the Mediterranean.

Supt. What kind of a country was this land of Moriah, when Abraham made an offering of his son Isaac on or in the vicinity of this mountain?

Same Pupil. It was a wild and wooded region.

Supt. Many years after, in the time of David, what was this place called, and what about it?

Same Pupil. It was called the "threshing-floor of Araunah, the Jebusite;" and David raised an altar there, when the destroying hand of the angel was stayed.

Supt. What about it under Solomon?

Same Pupil. The Temple of Solomon was built on this mountain.

Supt. What temples have since stood on Mount Moriah?

Same Pupil. It has been occupied in succession by Jewish, Christian, Pagan, and Mohammedan temples. Mount Moriah is now crowned with the mosque of St. Omar. It stands where the rude altar of Abraham rose nearly 4,000 years ago, where, years afterward, the temple of Solomon rose in all its splendor, and the Children of Israel paid their vows there: but it has no memorial like that of the offering up of Isaac.

MOUNT HOREB.

Supt. At what mountain did God appear in the burning bush to Moses?

Fourth Pupil. At Mount Horeb: "Now Moses kept the flock of Jethro, his father-in-law, the priest of Midian; and he led the flock to the back side of the desert, and came to the mountain of God, even to Horeb."—Ex. 3: 1.

Fifth Pupil. "And the angel of the Lord appeared unto him in a flame of fire, out of the midst of a bush; and he looked, and behold the bush burned with fire, and the bush was not consumed."—Ex. 3: 2.

Supt. What other miracle did Moses afterward witness at Horeb?

Sixth Pupil. The water brought from the dry rock: "Behold I will stand before thee there, upon the rock in Horeb; and thou shalt smite the rock, and there shall come water out of it, that the people may drink. And Moses did so in the sight of the elders of Israel."—Ex. 17: 6.

Bible Class Pupil. (Map Lesson.) Mount Horeb, one of the group that surrounds Sinai, has not only been consecrated once, but thrice, and hence has a three-fold claim for a place in the immortal list of *sacred mountains.* First, Moses, an exile from Egypt, while keeping the flocks of his father-in-law, saw here the burning bush, and received his first commission from God. Afterwards, the leader of a mighty people, Moses here saw the water gush forth from the smitten rock. Long years afterward, God revealed himself here to Elijah in the "still, small voice," after the wind, and the earthquake, and the fire.

MOUNT SINAI.

Supt. Where were the commandments delivered to Moses?

Seventh Pupil. Upon Mount Sinai: "And the Lord came down upon Mount Sinai, on the top of the Mount: and the Lord called Moses up to the top of the Mount, and Moses went up."—Ex. 19: 20.

Eighth Pupil. "And he gave unto Moses, when he had made an end of communing with him upon Mount Sinai, two tables of testimony, tables of stone, written with the finger of God."—Ex. 31: 18.

Supt. Where is Mount Sinai referred to as a type of the law, by which no man is justified?

Ninth Pupil. In Paul to the Hebrews, 12: 18, 19—"For ye are not come unto the mount that might be touched, and that burned with fire, nor unto blackness, and darkness, and tempest, and the sound of a trumpet, and the voice of words; which voice they that heard entreated that the word should not be spoken to them any more."

Bible Class Pupil. (Map Lesson.) The name Sinai, signifying "a district of broken rocks," is applied to a whole group of mountains in the peninsula formed by the northern gulfs of the Red Sea, but especially to one very lofty range, of which the northern end is termed Horeb, the southern Sinai, now called by the Arabs "*Jebel Musa*," or "Moses' Mount." It is a wild, desolate region of granite peaks and precipices, deep ravines and water-courses. The height of Sinai is above 7,000 feet, and the length of the whole range three miles.

Supt. What is one remarkable feature?

Same Pupil. "One remarkable feature of the district is the number of inscriptions on the rocks, so numerous in one place as to give it the name of the 'written valley.' It is hoped that when modern research has found how to decipher these, much light may be cast by them on Scripture history."

Supt. What is the scenery of Mount Sinai?

Same Pupil. It stands in the midst of some of the most desolate scenery in the world. Its bald and naked summit, its barren and rocky sides, and all its sombre features, correspond perfectly with the surrounding scene.

Supt. What is its sacred association?

Same Pupil. The exhibition of God in giving his law to man.

Supt. Consecrated by Jehovah's feet, and baptized by the cloud of fire and of glory, Mount Sinai stood the third *sacred mountain* on the earth.

MOUNT HOR.

Supt. On what mountain did Aaron die?

Tenth Pupil. Aaron died on Mount Hor: "And Moses did as the Lord commanded: and they went up into Mount Hor in the sight of all the congregation."—Num. 20: 27.

Eleventh Pupil. "And Moses stripped Aaron of his garments and put them upon Eleazar, his son; and Aaron died there, in the top of the mount; and Moses and Eleazar came down from the mount."—Num. 20: 28.

Bible Class Pupil. (Map Lesson.) "Mount Hor is a lonely peak, seen at a great distance from the desert, and constitutes one of the land-marks by which the Arab guides his way. On its summit is a white building called the 'Tomb of Aaron.' A land-mark in the bleak scenery, within sight of the desolate city of Edom, its pillared rocks overlook the Dead Sea."

MOUNT PISGAH.

Supt. On what mountain did Moses die?

Twelfth Pupil. He died on Mount Pisgah or Nebo: "And Moses went up from the plains of Moab, unto the Mountains of Nebo, to the top of Pisgah, that is over against Jericho; and the Lord shewed him all the land of Gilead, unto Dan."—Deut. 34: 1.

Thirteenth Pupil. "So Moses, the servant of the Lord, died there, in the land of Moab, according to the word of the Lord." Deut. 34: 5.

Bible Class Pupil. (Map Lesson.) Pisgah, a mountain ridge north and east of the Dead Sea. Nebo was one of its summits. Moses, like Aaron, was denied entrance into the land of Canaan. Here, in the top of Mount Nebo, Moses died, alone, and God buried him.

By Nebo's lonely mountain,
On this side Jordan's wave,
In a vale in the land of Moab,
There lies a lonely grave.
And no man knows that sepulchre,
And no man saw it e'er,
For the angels of God upturned the sod,
And laid the dead man there.

Yet from that summit of Pisgah he was permitted to view the goodly land, but the valley and river of Jordan lay between the dying prophet and the promised possession.

The Christian may, sometimes, from its spiritual heights, look beyond the dark river to the fair fields on the other side.

Singing "Pisgah's Mountain."—Fresh Laurels, p. 78.

MOUNT LEBANON.

Supt. What mountain of the promised land did Moses long to see before his death?

Thirteenth Pupil. Mount Lebanon: "I pray thee, let me go over and see the good land that is beyond Jordan, that goodly mountain and Lebanon."—Deut. 3: 25.

Supt. For what was Mount Lebanon distinguished?

Fourteenth Pupil. For its cedar and fir trees: "I am come up to the height of the mountains, to the sides of Lebanon, and will cut down the tall cedar trees thereof, and the choice fir trees thereof."—2 Kings 19: 23.

Supt. How is the fruitfulness of this mountain used in a figure, as a promise to God's people?

Fifteenth Pupil. "The righteous shall flourish like the palm-tree; he shall grow like a cedar in Lebanon."—Ps. 92: 12.

Bible Class Pupil. (Map Lesson.) Lebanon *means* white—a long chain of mountains. It consists of two ridges; the western is generally higher than the eastern, and several of its peaks are thought to be towards 10,000 feet high. An Arab poet says of the highest point of Lebanon, "He bears winter upon his head, spring upon his shoulders, and autumn in his bosom, while summer lies sleeping at his feet."

"From the sea Lebanon is still glorious to behold. The great landmark of that country, it stands unwasted by the ravages of time, and so long as the Bible remains, Lebanon shall stand as one of its witnesses."

MOUNT TABOR.

Supt. What mountain is supposed to have been the place of the transfiguration of Jesus?

Sixteenth Pupil. It is supposed to have been Mount Tabor: "And after six days Jesus taketh with him Peter, and James, and John, and leadeth them up into a high mountain, apart by themselves; and he was transfigured before them."—Mark 9: 2.

Seventeenth Pupil. "And his raiment became shining, exceeding white as snow; so as no fuller on earth can white them."—Mark 9: 3.

Bible Class Pupil. (Map Lesson.) Tabor is a beautiful mountain in the plain of Esdraelon, south from Nazareth. It rises abruptly to the height of a thousand feet. This is the same mountain on which Bonaparte fought the battle of Mount

Tabor, fifty years ago. How great are the contrasts of earth! Roll back twenty centuries, and the Saviour of the world stands here in the wondrous scene of the transfiguration.

MOUNT OLIVET.

Supt. What mountain was a favorite resort of Jesus with his disciples?

Eighteenth Pupil. Mount of Olives: "And he came out and went, as he was wont, to the Mount of Olives; and his disciples also followed him."—Luke 22: 39.

Supt. Did Jesus ever visit this mountain alone?

Nineteenth Pupil. He did: "And when he had sent the multitudes away, he went up into a mountain apart to pray; and when the evening was come he was there alone."—Matt. 14: 23.

Supt. Was this the Mount of Ascension?

Twentieth Pupil. It was: "And when he had spoken these things, while they beheld, he was taken up; and a cloud received him out of their sight."—Acts 1: 9.

Twenty-first Pupil. "Then returned they unto Jerusalem from the Mount called Olivet, which is from Jerusalem a Sabbath-day's journey."—Acts 1: 12.

Bible Class Pupil. (Map Lesson.) This is one of "the mountains round about Jerusalem." The burying ground of the Jews is here. Travelers often speak of the *beautiful Mount of Olives.*

Its associations are most tender and affecting. David fled hither from his rebellious son Absalom: "He went up by the ascent of Mount Olivet, and wept as he went up" (2 Sam. 15: 30); and here in later days, "king David's greater Son" ofttimes resorted for meditation and prayer. Here was the place of his lamentation over Jerusalem, and here was Gethsemane. Here he was betrayed with a kiss by one disciple, and forsaken by all the rest; and from this mount he ascended to heaven.

MOUNT CALVARY.

Supt. On what mount was Jesus crucified?

Twenty-second Pupil. On Mount Calvary: "And when they were come to the place which is called Calvary, there they crucified him, and the malefactors, one on the right hand and the other on the left."—Luke 23 : 33.

Ass't Supt. or a Teacher. It is the *atonement* that makes Mount Calvary chief among the *sacred mountains*—gives it such altitude that no mortal eye can scan its top.

Paul called on his young disciples to summon their strongest energies, and bend their highest efforts to comprehend the "length, and breadth, and depth, and height" of this stupendous theme—a length which reaches from everlasting to everlasting; a breadth that encompasses every intelligence and every interest; a depth which reaches the lowest state of human degradation and misery; and a height that throws floods of glory on the throne and crown of Jehovah.

Supt. How are the mountains named as a symbol of protection?

Teacher. "As the mountains are round about Jerusalem, so the Lord is round about his people from henceforth, even forever."—Ps. 125 : 2.

Supt. How as a symbol of stability?

Teacher. "They that trust in the Lord shall be as Mount Zion, which cannot be removed, but abideth forever."—Ps. 125 : 1.

Supt. How as a symbol of magnitude?

Teacher. "Thy righteousness is like the great mountains; thy judgments are a great deep. O Lord, thou preservest man and beast."—Ps. 36 : 6.

Supt. How are they named as a source of hope and help?

Teacher. "And I will lift mine eyes unto the hills, from whence cometh my help."—Ps. 121 : 2.

Another. "My help cometh from the Lord, which made heaven and earth."—Ps. 121 : 1.

Another. "How beautiful upon the mountains are the feet of him that bringeth good tidings, that publisheth peace; that bringeth good tidings of good, that publisheth salvation: that saith unto Zion, Thy God reigneth!"—Isaiah 52 : 7.

A Lady Teacher.

For the strength of the hills we bless thee,
  Our God, our fathers' God!
Thou hast made thy children mighty,
  By the touch of the mountain sod.
Thou hast fixed our ark of refuge
  Where the spoiler's foot ne'er trod;
For the strength of the hills we bless thee,
  Our God, our fathers' God!

MOUNT ZION.

Supt. What mountain near Mount Moriah was the home of David, and an accepted type of the church of God?

Teacher. It was Mount Zion: "Beautiful for situation, the joy of the whole earth, is Mount Zion, on the sides of the north, the city of the Great King."—Ps. 48 : 2.

Supt. As Mount Sinai was referred to as a type of the law, how is Mount Zion named as a type of Christ?

Member of Bible Class. "But ye are come unto Mount Zion, and unto the city of the living God, the heavenly Jerusalem, and to an innumerable company of angels."—Heb. 12 : 22.

Another. "To the general assembly and church of the First-born, which are written in heaven, and to God the judge of all, and to the spirits of just men made perfect."—Heb. 12 : 23.

Another. "And to Jesus the Mediator of the new covenant, and to the blood of sprinkling, that speaketh better things than that of Abel."—Heb. 12 : 24.

Supt. or Pastor. There is no name in history the mention of which awakens so many thrilling associations as that of Zion. It not only represents the ancient Jewish church, and all that was dear and holy in her, but it is applied to the Christian church of the present day. Confined to no sect, and no clime, and no language, it embraces in its catholicity all who love God, binding them in one endearing name together to the end of time.

The literal Mount Zion was one of the hills on which Jerusalem was built. But that prophecy has long since been fulfilled that told of its desolation.

There is a mount Zion in heaven, and the redeemed are there, and the song they sing has no dying cadence. The top of this heavenly mount is crowned with a more glorious temple than ever adorned an earthly city, and nothing that "can hurt or make afraid" shall ever enter there.

Ararat, with the heaven-lifted, heaven-guided ark resting on its summit, is but a symbol of the Christian's repose, after the storms of life, on the serene heights of perpetual bliss. Mount Moriah is only the shadow of that height of mystery where God offered up his Only Son, and there was no hand to stay the stroke. Sinai and Horeb are but dim reflections of the terrors of God's law. Mount Pisgah points to a "land of promise," from whose bosom rise more glorious summits than the "goodly mountain Lebanon." Olivet and Calvary are both eloquent of heaven. Tabor reveals, beforehand, the appearance which the Lamb of God will present when he stands on Mount Zion with the redeemed about him. That heavenly Mount Zion! All the ransomed of the Lord will be there. Aaron went up thither from the top of Hor, and Moses from Pisgah. Elijah's chariot of fire tarried not till it rested on that heavenly mount, and thither Christ ascended from the hill of Olives.

And thus the redeemed have flocked, one after another, to the Mount of God, and there they shall continue to gather, until the glorious assembly stands complete, and "God is all and in all."

Closing Song. "Beautiful Zion," verses 1, 2, and 4.—Happy Voices, p. 213. Or "My Home is There." —Fresh Laurels, p. 94.

VII.

Prayer:

A LESSON OF DEVOTION.

"Pray without ceasing."—1 *Thes.* 5: 17.

"And ye shall seek me and find me when ye shall search for me with all your heart."—*Jer.* 29: 13.

EXERCISE.

Opening Chant. The Lord's Prayer. (*See Appendix.*)

Singing. "Sweet Hour of Prayer."

Supt. "The Lord is nigh unto all them that call upon him, to all that call upon him in truth."

School. "And all things whatsoever ye shall ask in prayer, believing, ye shall receive."

Supt. "As for me, I will call upon God, and the Lord shall save me."

School. "For thou, Lord, art good, and ready to forgive, and plenteous in mercy unto all them that call upon thee."

PRAYER.

Scripture Reading. 40th Psalm.

Singing. "Jacob's Prayer."—Fresh Laurels, p. 92.

CLASS A.

Supt. What was the first prayer recorded in the Bible?

First Pupil. "And Abraham said unto God, Oh that Ishmael might live before thee!"—Gen. 17: 18.

Supt. Was it answered?

Second Pupil. It was. God said: "And as for Ishmael, I have heard thee: Behold I have blessed him. * * * I will make him a great nation."—Gen. 17: 20.

Supt. Repeat the prayer of Moses in behalf of Israel.

Third Pupil. "And Moses returned unto the Lord, and said. Oh, this people have sinned a great sin, and have made them gods of gold. Yet now, if thou wilt forgive their sin —; and if not, blot me, I pray thee, out of thy book, which thou hast written."— Ex. 32: 31, 32.

Supt. What did Solomon ask of God?

Fourth Pupil. "And now, O Lord my God, thou hast made thy servant king instead of David my father: and I am but a little child: I know not how to go out or come in. And thy servant is in the midst of thy people which thou hast chosen, a great people, that cannot be numbered nor counted for multitude. Give therefore thy servant an understanding heart to judge thy people, that I may discern between good and bad: for who is able to judge this thy so great a people?"— 1 Kings 3: 7–9.

Supt. What was the prayer of Elijah at Carmel?

Fifth Pupil. "Now therefore send, and gather to me all Israel unto mount Carmel, and the prophets of Baal four hundred and fifty, and the prophets of the groves four hundred, which eat at Jezebel's table."

"Hear me, O Lord, hear me, that this people may know that thou art the Lord God, and that thou hast turned their heart back again."— 1 Kings 18: 19, 37.

Singing. "Watch and Pray."— Fresh Laurels, p. 54.

Supt. Class B repeat Daniel's prayer of thanksgiving and praise. (Daniel 2: 20–24.)

First Pupil. "Daniel answered and said, Blessed be the name of God for ever and ever: for wisdom and might are his."

Second Pupil. "And he changeth the times and the seasons: he removeth kings, and setteth up kings: he giveth wisdom unto the wise, and knowledge to them that know understanding:"

Third Pupil. "He revealeth the deep and secret things: he knoweth what is in the darkness, and the light dwelleth with him."

Fourth Pupil. "I thank thee, and praise thee, O thou God of my fathers, who hast given me wisdom and might, and hast made known unto me now what we desired of thee: for thou hast now made known unto us the king's matter."

Supt. CLASS C will repeat some of David's prayers.

First Pupil. "Unto thee will I cry, O Lord my rock; be not silent to me: lest, if thou be silent to me, I become like them that go down into the pit."—Ps. 28: 1.

Second Pupil. "Hear the voice of my supplications, when I cry unto thee, when I lift up my hands toward thy holy oracle."—Ps. 28: 2.

Third Pupil. "Be merciful unto me, O God, be merciful unto me: for my soul trusteth in thee: yea, in the shadow of thy wings will I make my refuge."—Ps. 57: 1.

Fourth Pupil. "Give ear, O Lord, unto my prayer; and attend to the voice of my supplications. In the day of my trouble I will call upon thee: for thou wilt answer me."——Ps. 86: 6, 7.

Fifth Pupil. "As for me, I will call upon God, and the Lord shall save me."—Ps. 55: 16.

Sixth Pupil. "Evening and morning, and at noon, will I pray and cry aloud; and he shall hear my voice."—Ps. 55: 17.

Supt. What was David's prayer for a revival of religion?

Teacher. "Turn us again, O God, and cause thy face to shine; and we shall be saved. O Lord God of hosts, how long wilt thou be angry against the prayer of thy people?"—Ps. 80: 3, 4.

RECITATION.

1 My God, is any hour so sweet,
From blush of morn to evening star,
As that which calls me to thy feet,
The hour of prayer?
Blest is that tranquil hour of morn,
And blest that hour of solemn eve,
When on the wings of faith upborne,
The world I leave.

2 Pray, though the gift you ask for
May never comfort your fears,
May never repay your pleading,
Yet pray, and with hopeful tears.
An answer — not that you sought for,
But diviner — will come one day:
Your eyes are too dim to see it,
Yet strive and wait and pray. *C. Elliott.*

Supt. Repeat the prayer of the Pharisee and Publican.

Bible Class Pupil. "The Pharisee stood and prayed thus with himself: God, I thank thee that I am not as other men are, extortioners, unjust, adulterers, or even as this Publican: I fast twice in the week, I give tithes of all that I possess."

"And the Publican, standing afar off, would not lift up so much as his eyes unto heaven; but smote upon his breast, saying, God be merciful to me a sinner."—Luke 18: 11–13.

Supt. Which prayer was acceptable; and why?

Another. The latter. "The sacrifices of God are a broken spirit. A broken and a contrite heart O God thou wilt not despise."—Ps. 51: 17.

Supt. What was Paul's first prayer?

Another. "And he trembling and astonished said, Lord, what wilt thou have me to do?"—Acts 9: 6, first clause.

Supt. What was Stephen's dying prayer?

Another. "And they stoned Stephen calling upon God and saying, Lord Jesus, receive my spirit. And he kneeled down and cried with a loud voice, Lord, lay not this sin to their charge. And when he had said this, he fell asleep."—Acts 7: 59, 60.

Supt. What did Christ ask for his disciples?

Another. "Neither pray I for these alone; but for them also which shall believe on me through their word: that they all may be one; as thou Father art in me, and I in thee, that they also may be one in us: that the world may believe that thou hast sent me."—John 17: 20, 21.

Supt. What was Christ's prayer on the cross?

Another. "Then said Jesus, Father, forgive them: for they know not what they do."—Luke 23: 34, first clause.

RECITATION.

1 O Thou, the contrite sinner's friend,
Who, loving, lov'st them to the end;
On this alone my hopes depend,
That thou wilt plead for me.

2 When, weary in the Christian race,
Far off appears my resting place,
And, fainting, I mistrust thy grace,
Then, Saviour, plead for me.

3 When I have erred and gone astray,
Afar from thine and wisdom's way,
And see no glimmering, guiding ray,
Still, Saviour, plead for me!

4 When Satan, by my sins made bold,
Strives from thy cross to loose my hold,
Then with thy pitying arms enfold
And plead, oh, plead for me!

Supt. How are *we* taught to pray?

CLASS D.

First Pupil. IN CHRIST'S NAME. "Verily, verily, I say unto you, Whatsoever ye shall ask the Father in my name, he will give it you."—John 16: 23.

Second Pupil. IN FAITH. "Trust in him at all times; ye people, pour out your heart before him: God is a refuge for us." —Ps. 62: 8.

Third Pupil. IN SINCERITY. "And ye shall seek me, and find me, when ye shall search for me with all your heart."—Jer. 29: 13.

Fourth Pupil. IN RIGHTEOUSNESS. "For the eyes of the Lord are over the righteous, and his ears are open unto their prayers; but the face of the Lord is against them that do evil." —1 Peter 3: 12.

Fifth Pupil. IN HUMILITY AND PATIENCE. "He forgetteth not the cry of the humble."—Ps. 9: 12.

"I waited patiently for the Lord, and he inclined unto me and heard my cry."—Ps. 40: 1.

Sixth Pupil. WITH CONFESSION AND FORGIVENESS. "And when ye stand praying, forgive, if ye have aught against any; that your Father also which is in heaven may forgive you your trespasses."—Mark 11 : 25.

Seventh Pupil. WITH PERSEVERANCE. "And he spake a parable unto them to this end, that men ought always to pray and not to faint."—Luke 18 : 1.

RECITATION.

1 Prayer is the soul's sincere desire,
Uttered or unexpressed;
The motion of a hidden fire
That trembles in the breast.

2 Prayer is the burden of a sigh,
The falling of a tear,
The upward glancing of an eye,
When none but God is near.

3 Prayer is the Christian's vital breath,
The Christian's native air,
His watchword at the gates of death;
He enters heaven with prayer.

4 Prayer is the contrite sinner's voice
Returning from his ways,
While angels in their songs rejoice,
And cry, "Behold, he prays."

5 O thou by whom we come to God,
The Life, the Truth, the Way,
The path of prayer thyself hast trod;
Lord teach *us* how to pray. *Montgomery.*

Singing. "I love to steal awhile away."

Supt. For what should we pray?

First Teacher. FOR CONVICTION OF SIN. "How many are mine iniquities and sins? make me to know my transgression and my sin."—Job 13 : 23.

Second Teacher. FOR REGENERATION. "Create in me a clean heart, O God; and renew a right spirit within me."—Ps. 51 : 10.

Third Teacher. FOR PARDON. "For thy name's sake, O Lord, pardon mine iniquity: for it is great."—Ps. 25 : 11.

Fourth Teacher. FOR KNOWLEDGE OF DIVINE THINGS. "Lead me in thy truth and teach me; for thou art the God of my salvation: on thee do I wait all the day."— Ps. 25: 5.

Fifth Teacher. FOR SANCTIFICATION. "Hold thou me up and I shall be safe: and I will have respect unto thy statutes continually."— Ps. 119: 117.

Sixth Teacher. FOR BLESSING UPON FOOD. "And when he had thus spoken, he took bread and gave thanks to God in presence of them all, and when he had broken it, he began to eat."— Acts 27: 35.

Supt. Are we taught to intercede for others?

Seventh Teacher. "Confess your faults one to another, and pray one for another, that ye may be healed. The effectual, fervent prayer of a righteous man availeth much."—James 5: 16.

Eighth Teacher. "But I say unto you, love your enemies, bless them that curse you, and pray for them which despitefully use you, and persecute you."— Matt. 5: 44.

Supt. Can we be sure that God hears the prayers of each one of us?

Ninth Teacher. "*Every one that asketh* receiveth; and *he that seeketh* findeth; and *to him that knocketh* it shall be opened." —Luke 11: 10.

Tenth Teacher. "Call unto me and I will answer thee and shew thee great and mighty things which thou knowest not." —Jer. 33: 3.

Eleventh Teacher. "Come unto me all ye that labor and are heavy laden, and I will give you rest."—Matt. 11: 28.

Singing. "Olivet."

My faith looks up to thee,
Thou Lamb of Calvary.

Brief Remarks by the Pastor, closing with prayer and

THE "MOSAIC BENEDICTION."

"The Lord bless thee, and keep thee: the Lord make his face shine upon thee, and be gracious unto thee: the Lord lift up his countenance upon thee, and give thee peace."

VIII.

Our Saviour:

A LESSON FOR CHRISTMAS.

"Glory to God in the highest, and on earth peace, good will toward men."—*Luke* 2: 14.

"Herein is love,—not that we loved God, but that he loved us, and sent his Son to be a propitiation for our sins."—1 *John* 4: 10.

EXERCISE.

Opening Hymn. Congregation sing:

Hail to the brightness of Zion's glad morning.

A Pupil from the platform recites the following

ANNOUNCEMENT.

"Fear not; for behold I bring you good tidings of great joy, which shall be to all people; for unto you is born this day, in the city of David, a Saviour which is Christ the Lord."

Congregation sing responsively:

Joy to the world; the Lord is come!
  Let earth receive her King;
Let every heart prepare him room,
  And every creature sing.

A Little Boy, standing in front, repeats reverently the following prayer:

Grant thy blessing, Lord, we pray,
On this happy Christmas Day;
May we love to read thy word;
May we try to serve thee, Lord;
All our sins do thou forgive;
May we fear thee while we live:
Jesus—Saviour! on us shine,
Make our hearts entirely thine.

Congregation sing promptly in response (tune as above):

Let the whole earth his love proclaim,
  With all her diff'rent tongues,
And spread the honor of his name,
  In melody and songs.

Superintendent reads the Scriptures; Luke 2: 1–14.

Congregation respond:

No more let sin and sorrow grow,
  Nor thorns infest the ground;
He comes to make his blessings flow
  Far as the curse is found.

Assistant Superintendent reads the Scriptures; Isa. 9: 6, 7.

Congregation respond:

He rules the world in truth and peace,
  And makes the nations prove
The glories of his righteousness,
  And wonders of his love.

RECITATION

By three scholars from Infant Department:

First Pupil. Though but little children,
  Poor and weak are we,
Yet this holy season
  Not unmarked shall be.
And our Christmas Carol,
  We will gladly raise,
To our Heavenly Father,
  Giving thanks and praise.

Second Pupil. Suffer little children,
  Did our Saviour say;
From our small endeavor
  He'll not turn away;
And he suffered for us
  Grief and pain and loss,
Till at last they nailed him
  On the awful cross.

Third Pupil. Honor, praise, and glory,
  To our Heavenly King
Now, and still forever,
  All mankind shall sing.
We will raise our Carol,
  As we gladly say:
Jesus Christ, our Saviour,
  He was born to-day.

Singing. "On a Christmas Morning."—Golden Shower, p. 6.

SONG.

Teachers. Children, can you truly tell,
Do you know the story well,
Every girl and every boy,
Why the angels sing for joy?
CHORUS, *by all*—On the Christmas morning,
The angels sing for joy.

Children. Yes, we know the story well,
Listen, now, and hear us tell,
Every girl and every boy,
Why the angels sing for joy
CHORUS—On the Christmas morning.

Children. Shepherds sat upon the ground,
Fleecy flocks were scattered round,
When the brightness filled the sky,
And a song was heard on high,
CHORUS—On the Christmas morning.

Children. "Joy and peace" the angels sang,
Far the pleasant echoes rang;
"Peace on earth, to men good will:"
Hark! the angels sing it still,
CHORUS—On the Christmas morning.

Children. "Peace" our every heart shall fill,
"Peace on earth, to men good will:"
Hear us sing the angels' song,
And the pleasant notes prolong
CHORUS—On the Christmas morning.

THE LESSON.

Supt. A Saviour promised.

First Pupil. "And the Lord God said unto the serpent, Because thou hast done this, thou art cursed above all cattle, and above every beast of the field: upon thy belly shalt thou go, and dust shalt thou eat all the days of thy life;"—Gen. 3: 14.

Second Pupil. "And I will put enmity between thee and the woman, and between thy seed and her seed: it shall bruise thy head, and thou shalt bruise his heel."—Gen. 3: 15.

8

Third Pupil. "The sceptre shall not depart from Judah, nor a law-giver from between his feet, until Shiloh come; and unto Him shall the gathering of the people be."—Gen. 49: 10.

Supt. The covenant and promise.

Fourth Pupil. "Now the Lord had said unto Abram, Get thee out of thy country, and from thy kindred, and from thy father's house, unto a land that I will show thee: and I will make of thee a great nation, and I will bless thee, and make thy name great; and thou shalt be a blessing."—Gen. 12: 1, 2.

Fifth Pupil. "And I will bless them that bless thee, and curse him that curseth thee: and in thee shall all families of the earth be blessed."—Gen. 12: 3.

Sixth Pupil. "I have made a covenant with my chosen, I have sworn unto David my servant."—Ps. 89: 3.

Seventh Pupil. "His seed shall endure forever, and his throne as the sun before me."—Ps. 89: 36.

Eighth Pupil. "Behold, the days come, saith the Lord, that I will raise unto David a righteous Branch, and a King shall reign and prosper, and shall execute judgment and justice in the earth."—Jer. 23: 5.

Ninth Pupil. "Therefore the Lord himself shall give you a sign: Behold, a virgin shall conceive and bear a son, and shall call his name Immanuel."—Isa. 7: 14.

Tenth Pupil. "Behold, the Lord hath proclaimed unto the end of the world, Say ye to the daughter of Zion, Behold, thy salvation cometh; behold, his reward is with him, and his work is before him."—Isa. 62: 11.

Eleventh Pupil. "But thou, Bethlehem Ephratah, though thou be little among the thousands of Judah, yet out of thee shall he come forth unto me that is to be Ruler in Israel; whose goings forth have been from of old, from everlasting."—Micah 5: 2.

Twelfth Pupil. "And Herod, when he had gathered all the chief priests and scribes of the people together, demanded of them where Christ should be born. And they said unto him, In Bethlehem of Judea: for thus it is written by the prophet." —Matt. 2: 4, 5.

Thirteenth Pupil. "And thou Bethlehem, in the land of Juda, art not the least among the princes of Juda: for out of thee shall come a governor, that shall rule my people Israel." —Matt. 2: 6.

Supt. The record of the Saviour's birth—prophecy fulfilled.

Fourteenth Pupil. "And in the sixth month the angel Gabriel was sent from God, unto a city of Galilee, named Nazareth,"—Luke 1: 26.

Fifteenth Pupil. "To a virgin espoused to a man whose name was Joseph, of the house of David; and the virgin's name was Mary."—Luke 1: 27.

Sixteenth Pupil. "And the angel came in unto her, and said, Hail, thou that art highly favored, the Lord is with thee: blessed art thou among women."—Luke 1: 28.

Seventeenth Pupil. "And the angel answered and said unto her, the Holy Ghost shall come upon thee, and the power of the Highest shall overshadow thee; therefore also that holy thing which shall be born of thee shall be called the Son of God." —Luke 1: 35.

Nineteenth Pupil. "And it came to pass in those days, that there went out a decree from Cæsar Augustus, that all the world should be taxed."—Luke 2: 1.

Twentieth Pupil. "And all went to be taxed, every one into his own city."—Luke 2: 3.

Twenty-first Pupil. "And Joseph also went up from Galilee, out of the city of Nazareth, into Judea, unto the city of David, which is called Bethlehem (because he was of the house and lineage of David)."—Luke 2: 4.

Twenty-second Pupil. "And she brought forth her first-born son, and wrapped him in swaddling clothes, and laid him in a manger; because there was no room for them in the inn."—Luke 2: 7.

Teacher, or member of young ladies' Bible Class:

Pillowed is his infant head
On a borrowed manger-bed!
He around whose throne above
Angels hymned their songs of love,
Now is wrapped by virgin hands
In earth's meanest swaddling bands:
Once adored by seraphim!
Now a babe of Bethlehem.

Supt. "The great Architect of the universe now dwells in a manger, and he who clothed himself with light, as with a garment, is now arrayed in the swaddling clothes of mortality, bone of our bone, and flesh of our flesh."

Song. "Christmas Carol."—The Charm, p. 145.

1 There's a song in the air!
There's a star in the sky!
There's a mother's deep prayer
And a baby's low cry!
And the star rains its fire while the beautiful sing,
For the manger of Bethlehem cradles a King.
Jesus is King, Jesus is King,
For the manger of Bethlehem cradles a King.

2 There's a tumult of joy
O'er the wonderful birth,
For the Virgin's sweet boy
Is the Lord of the earth.
Ay! the star rains its fire, and the beautiful sing,
For the manger of Bethlehem cradles a King.
Jesus is King, etc.

3 In the light of that star
Lie the ages impearled,
And that song from afar
Has swept over the world.
Every hearth is a flame, and the beautiful sing,
In the homes of the nations that Jesus is King.

4 We rejoice in the light,
And we echo the song
That comes down through the night
From the heavenly throng.
Ay! we shout to the lovely evangel they bring,
And we greet in his cradle our Saviour and King.

Supt. The announcement to the shepherds.

Twenty-third Pupil. "And there were in the same country shepherds abiding in the field, keeping watch over their flock by night."—Luke 2: 8.

Twenty-fourth Pupil. "And lo, the angel of the Lord came upon them, and the glory of the Lord shone round about them, and they were sore afraid."—Luke 2: 9.

Twenty-fifth Pupil. "And the angel said unto them, Fear not: for behold, I bring you good tidings of great joy, which shall be to all people."—Luke 2 : 10.

Twenty-sixth Pupil. "For unto you is born this day, in the city of David, a Saviour, which is Christ the Lord."—Luke 2 : 11.

Twenty-seventh Pupil. "And this shall be a sign unto you: Ye shall find the babe wrapped in swaddling clothes, lying in a manger."—Luke 2 : 12.

Twenty-eighth Pupil. "And suddenly there was with the angel a multitude of the heavenly host, praising God, and saying,"—Luke 2 : 13.

Twenty-ninth Pupil. "Glory to God in the highest, and on earth peace, good will toward men."—Luke 2 : 14.

Supt. What of the wise men from the East?

Thirtieth Pupil. "Now when Jesus was born in Bethlehem of Judea, in the days of Herod the King, behold, there came wise men from the east to Jerusalem."—Matt. 2 : 1.

Thirty-first Pupil. "Saying, Where is he that is born King of the Jews? for we have seen his star in the east, and are come to worship him."—Matt. 2 : 2.

Thirty-second Pupil. "When they saw the star, they rejoiced with exceeding great joy."—Matt. 2 : 10.

Thirty-third Pupil. "And when they were come into the house, they saw the young child with Mary his mother, and fell down, and worshipped him; and when they had opened their treasures, they presented unto him gifts; gold, and frankincense, and myrrh."—Matt. 2 : 11.

Singing. "Christmas Hymn"—duet and chorus. —Happy Voices, p. 158.

Christ is born and heaven rejoices.

Or, "The Shepherds of Bethlehem."—The Charm, p. 138.

They are watching on the hillsides for the coming day.

Supt. What do we know of his childhood?

Thirty-fourth Pupil. "And the child grew, and waxed strong in spirit, filled with wisdom; and the grace of God was upon him."—Luke 2: 40.

Thirty-fifth Pupil. "And Jesus increased in wisdom and stature, and in favor with God and man."—Luke 2: 52.

Supt. Who attested to his divinity after he began his public ministry?

Thirty-sixth Pupil. "And there came a voice from heaven, saying, Thou art my beloved Son, in whom I am well pleased." —Mark 1: 11.

Thirty-seventh Pupil. "And John bare record, saying, I saw the spirit descending from heaven like a dove, and it abode upon him."—John 1: 32.

Supt. Why did he call himself the Son of Man?

Thirty-eighth Pupil. "For verily he took not on him the nature of angels; but he took on him the seed of Abraham."—Heb. 2: 16.

Thirty-ninth Pupil. "But made himself of no reputation, and took upon him the form of a servant, and was made in the likeness of men."—Phil. 2: 7.

Fortieth Pupil. "For there is one God, and one Mediator between God and men, the man Christ Jesus."—1 Tim. 2: 5.

A Teacher. "The vast extent between the finite and the infinite is now spanned over by the birth of Jesus. In the birth of Jesus our hope has birth. Why did he indeed robe himself in fleshly vestments, and cast away his glory for a time, but that he might clothe and beautify his people? Through his birth as a man he comes to us, that we, through a new birth, might be raised to him."

Supt. Was Christ God as well as man?

Forty-first Pupil. "Now all this was done, that it might be fulfilled which was spoken of the Lord by the prophet, saying, Behold, a virgin shall be with child, and shall bring forth a son, and they shall call his name Emmanuel; which being interpreted is, God with us."—Matt. 1: 22, 23.

Forty-second Pupil. "In the beginning was the Word, and the Word was with God, and the Word was God."—John 1: 1.

Forty-third Pupil. "I and my Father are one."—John 10 : 30.

Forty-fourth Pupil. "The first man is of the earth, earthy: the second man is the Lord from heaven."— 1 Cor. 15 : 47.

Forty-fifth Pupil. "I am Alpha and Omega, the beginning and the end, the first and the last."— Rev. 22 : 13.

Singing. "The Children's Te Deum."— Fresh Laurels, p. 104.

We praise thee, we bless thee, thou who only art divine.

Supt. The Saviour of sinners.

Forty-sixth Pupil. "Unto you is born this day, in the city of David, a Saviour, which is Christ the Lord."— Luke 2 : 11.

Forty-seventh Pupil. "This is a faithful saying, and worthy of all acceptation, that Christ Jesus came into the world to save sinners."— 1 Tim. 1 : 15.

Forty-eighth Pupil. "And we have seen, and do testify, that the Father sent the Son to be the Saviour of the world."— 1 John 4 : 14.

Supt. Do we all need such a Saviour?

Forty-ninth Pupil. "The Lord looked down from heaven upon the children of men, to see if there were any that did understand, and seek God. They are all gone aside, they are all together become filthy; there is none that doeth good, no, not one."— Ps. 14 : 2, 3.

Fiftieth Pupil. "If we say that we have no sin, we deceive ourselves, and the truth is not in us."— 1 John 1 : 8.

Fifty-first Pupil. "The soul that sinneth, it shall die."— Ezek. 18 : 4.

Fifty-second Pupil. "But God commendeth his love towards us, in that, while we were yet sinners, Christ died for us."— Rom. 5 : 8.

Fifty-third Pupil. "For he hath made him to be sin for us, who knew no sin; that we might be made the righteousness of God in him."— 2 Cor. 5 : 21.

Fifty-fourth Pupil. "Who his own self bare our sins in his own body on the tree, that we, being dead to sins, should live unto righteousness: by whose stripes ye were healed."—1 Peter 2: 24.

Fifty-fifth Pupil. "And as Moses lifted up the serpent in the wilderness, even so must the Son of Man be lifted up."—John 3: 14.

Fifty-sixth Pupil. "That whosoever believeth in him should not perish, but have eternal life."—John 3: 15.

Supt. "Reflect, then, O my soul, in thine own low estate, and utter helplessness. Remember the Saviour in the manger, and learn the lesson of redemption. He is beneath thee to lift thee up, and however high thou mayest rise, he is still above thee. Amid all life's changing scenes submissive bow, and say, Since Jesus to the manger came, thy will, O Lord, be done."

Asst. Supt. "Casting all your care upon him, for he careth for you."—1 Peter 5: 7.

Pastor. "For we have not an high priest which cannot be touched with the feeling of our infirmities: but was in all points tempted like as we are, yet without sin. Let us therefore come boldly unto the throne of grace, that we may obtain mercy, and find grace to help in time of need."—Heb. 4: 15, 16.

PRAYER BY PASTOR.

Singing. "Coronation."

IX.

The Lord's Prayer:

A LESSON FOR EVERY DAY IN THE YEAR.

"My voice shalt thou hear in the morning, O Lord; in the morning will I direct my prayer unto thee, and will look up."—*Ps.* 5: 3.

"After this manner, therefore, pray ye."—*Matt.* 6: 9.

EXERCISE.

Superintendent. "Oh come, let us worship and bow down; let us kneel before the Lord our Maker."

Recitation by Superintendent, and *Responsive Chant* by school, "The Lord's Prayer."—Notes of Joy, pp. 160, 161.

PRAYER.

(*Referring especially to the subject of the Exercise.*)

Singing. "Pray without Ceasing."—Notes of Joy, p. 29. Or, "Watch and Pray."—Fresh Laurels, p. 54.

INFANT CLASS RECITATION.

THE CHILD'S PRAYER.

1 Saviour, precious Saviour,
Ever meek and mild,
In thy tender mercy,
Hear a little child.
Teach me how to love thee,
Teach me how to pray;
Whisper to my spirit,
Tell me what to say.
Fold me on thy bosom,
Let me come to thee,
Little lamb of Jesus,
I would ever be.

2 Like a gentle shepherd,
Lead me all the day;
Saviour do not leave me,
Let me never stray.

When my steps are weary,
Lay me on thy breast;
Sweet will be my slumber,
Peaceful there my rest.
Fold me on thy bosom,
Let me come to thee;
Little lamb of Jesus,
I would ever be.

3 With a bird that carols,
In the pleasant shade,
With a stream that wanders,
In the summer glade;
Jesus, I would praise thee,
In my happy song;
Of thy loving kindness,
Singing all day long.
Fold me on thy bosom,
Let me come to thee;
Little lamb of Jesus,
I would ever be.

Supt. We are to study to-night "THE LORD'S PRAYER."

(*If possible, have the Prayer in large letters on a chart before the school, or plainly written on the blackboard.*)

The invocation is "OUR FATHER."

CLASS A.

First Pupil. God is our father, By right of creation,
By merit of mercy,
By bountiful providence.

Supt. How is God our father by right of creation?

Second Pupil. "And God said, Let us make man in our image, after our likeness. So God created man in his own image, in the image of God created he him; male and female created he them."—Gen. 1: 26, 27.

Supt. How is God our father by merit of mercy?

Third Pupil. "For God so loved the world that he gave his only begotten Son, that whosoever believeth in him should not perish, but have everlasting life."—John 3: 16.

Supt. How is God our father by bountiful providence?

Fourth Pupil. "Praise waiteth for thee, O God, in Zion; thou crownest the year with thy goodness. and thy paths drop fatness."—Ps 65: 1, 11.

Fifth Pupil. "The eyes of all wait upon thee, and thou givest them their meat in due season. Thou openest thine hand, and satisfiest the desire of every living thing."—Ps. 145: 15, 16.

Supt. God is our *father* and we are his *children.*

Class B.

First Pupil. "But now, O Lord, thou art our father: we are the clay, and thou our potter; and we all are the work of thy hand."—Isa. 64: 8.

Second Pupil. "Having predestinated us unto the adoption of children by Jesus Christ to himself, according to the good pleasure of his will."—Eph. 1: 5.

Third Pupil. "But love ye your enemies, and do good, and lend, hoping for nothing again; and your reward shall be great, and ye shall be the children of the Highest: for he is kind unto the unthankful and to the evil."—Luke 6: 35, 36.

Fourth Pupil. "Be ye therefore followers of God, as dear children."—Eph. 5: 1.

Supt. After the invocation, follows God's dwelling-place, "WHICH ART IN HEAVEN."

Class C.

First Pupil. The seat of thy majesty,
The home of thy children,
The kingdom of bliss.

Second Pupil. The seat of thy majesty: "Heaven is my throne, and earth is my footstool: what house will ye build me? saith the Lord: or what is the place of my rest?"—Acts 7: 49.

Third Pupil. The home of thy children: "An inheritance incorruptible, and undefiled, and that fadeth not away, reserved in heaven for you."—1 Peter 1: 4.

Fourth Pupil. The kingdom of bliss: "And there shall be no more curse: but the throne of God and of the Lamb shall be in it; and his servants shall serve him: and they shall see his face; and his name shall be in their foreheads."—Rev. 22: 3, 4.

Supt. Then follows the way in which God's children are to regard his name: "HALLOWED BE THY NAME."

CLASS D.

First Pupil. By our thoughts and our hearts,
By the words of our mouths,
By the works of our hands.

Second Pupil. "I will extol thee, my God, O King; and I will bless thy name for ever and ever. Every day will I bless thee; and I will praise thy name for ever and ever."—Ps. 145: 1, 2.

Third Pupil. "All nations whom thou hast made shall come and worship before thee, O Lord, and shall glorify thy name. For thou art great, and doest wondrous things: thou art God alone."—Ps. 86: 9, 10.

Fourth Pupil. "I will make thy name to be remembered in all generations: therefore shall the people praise thee for ever and ever."—Ps. 45: 17.

Fifth Pupil. "Commit thy works unto the Lord, and thy thoughts shall be established."—Prov. 16: 3.

Supt. Then follows the earnest wish of God's children, "THY KINGDOM COME."

CLASS E.

First Pupil. Of grace to inspire us,
Of power to defend us,
Of glory to crown us.

Supt. "THY WILL BE DONE."

Second Pupil. In weal and in woe,
In fulness and in want,
In life and in death.

Supt. "IN EARTH AS IN HEAVEN."

Third Pupil. In us as with angels,
Willingly, readily, faithfully,
Now and eternally.

Fourth Pupil. "And it shall come to pass in the last days, that the mountain of the Lord's house shall be established in the top of the mountains, and shall be exalted above the hills; and all nations shall flow unto it."— Isa. 2 : 2.

Fifth Pupil. "And blessed be his glorious name for ever: and let the whole earth be filled with his glory. Amen, and Amen."— Ps. 72 : 19.

Singing. "Awake, O Earth."— Notes of Joy, p. 131 (or substitute).

Supt. Then the *prayer* presents this humble but all-important request: "GIVE US THIS DAY OUR DAILY BREAD."

CLASS F.

First Pupil. For the nourishing of our bodies,
For the feeding of our souls,
For the relief of our necessities.

Second Pupil. The "wise man" said: "Remove far from me vanity and lies: give me neither poverty nor riches; feed me with food convenient for me."— Prov. 30 : 8.

Third Pupil. Christ said: "I am that bread of life."— John 6 : 48.

Supt. Next a supplication for pardon: "AND FORGIVE US OUR DEBTS AS WE FORGIVE OUR DEBTORS."

Fourth Pupil. Against the commands of the law,
Against the grace of thy gospel,
Against our neighbor and ourselves.

Fifth Pupil. "For if ye forgive men their trespasses, your heavenly Father will also forgive you."—Matt. 6 : 14.

Supt. Then follows the petition for guidance and protection: "LEAD US NOT INTO TEMPTATION."

Class G.

First Pupil. Of the wicked world,
Of the enticing flesh,
Of the spirit of evil.

Second Pupil. Christ said: "Watch and pray, that ye enter not into temptation: the spirit indeed is willing, but the flesh is weak."—Matt. 26: 41.

Supt. Then a cry for relief: "BUT DELIVER US FROM EVIL."

Third Pupil. Forgive what is past,
Reprove what is present,
Prevent what may come.

Fourth Pupil. "I pray not that thou shouldest take them out of the world, but that thou shouldest keep them from the evil."—John 17: 15.

Supt. Then an acknowledgment of God's sovereignty and omnipotence: "FOR THINE IS THE KINGDOM, AND THE POWER, AND THE GLORY."

Fifth Pupil. Thy kingdom governs all,
Thy power subdues all,
Thy glory is above all.

Sixth Pupil. "And after these things I heard a great voice of much people in heaven, saying, Alleluia; salvation, and glory, and honor, and power, unto the Lord our God."—Rev. 19: 1.

Seventh Pupil. "And every creature which is in heaven, and on the earth, and under the earth, and such as are in the sea, and all that are in them, heard I saying, Blessing, and honor, and glory, and power, be unto him that sitteth upon the throne, and unto the Lamb for ever and ever."—Rev. 5: 13.

Eighth Pupil. "Who only hath immortality, dwelling in the light which no man can approach unto; whom no man hath seen, nor can see: to whom be honor and power everlasting. Amen."—1 Tim. 6: 16.

Supt. And lastly, this beautiful and wonderful prayer closes with the desire for the *endless* enjoyment of God's dominion and glory: "FOR EVER AND EVER, AMEN."

A Teacher. In this short life,
In the endless *hereafter.*

Another. "Thy throne, O God, is for ever and ever: the sceptre of thy kingdom is a right sceptre."—Ps. 45 : 6.

Supt. This is the "*Lord's Prayer.*" He has given it to us for *our* prayer. Its instruction, its simplicity and comprehensiveness are wonderful. It shuts out selfishness, and teaches confidence and reverence, and inspires us with zeal and fidelity.

Singing. "Gloria in Excelsis." (*See Appendix.*)

BRIEF ADDRESS,

Relating to and impressing some practical point of the lesson.

Singing. "Notes of Joy," p. 116.

Our heavenly Father,
Hear the prayer we offer now.

BRIEF PRAYER AND BENEDICTION.

X.

The Sermon on the Mount:

A LESSON FROM THE WORDS OF CHRIST.

"Never man spake like this man."—*John* 7 : 46.

"These are written that ye might believe that Jesus is the Christ, the Son of God; and that believing ye might have life through his name."—*John* 20: 31.

EXERCISE.

Opening Song. "Gladly Meeting."—Fresh Laurels, p. 25.

Scripture Reading. The Superintendent reads from the beginning of the 6th chapter of Matthew to the second clause of the 9th verse, when the members of the school bow their heads, and unite with him in chanting, with organ accompaniment, The Lord's Prayer.

PRAYER BY THE PASTOR.

Singing. "The Pure in Heart."—Fresh Laurels, p. 46.

1 Blessed are the pure in heart!
Blessed evermore!
They shall meet, and never part
On the golden shore.
Thorny paths their feet have trod,
But their rest is sure with God!
CHORUS.—Blessed are the pure in heart,
Blessed are the pure in heart!
Blessed evermore,
Blessed evermore!

2 Blessed are the pure in heart,
Free from sin and stain:
Satan, with his fiery dart,
Tempts their peace in vain;
For they lean on Jesus' arm,
He will keep them safe from harm.
CHORUS.

3 Blessed are the pure in heart!
Oh! that we may stand,
Choosing now the better part
At the Lord's right hand.
With us may his love abide,
For the sake of Christ who died!

CHORUS.

Supt. Whom besides the pure in heart did Christ call blessed?

CLASS A.

First Pupil. "Blessed are the poor in spirit: for theirs is the kingdom of heaven."—Matt. 5: 3.

Second Pupil. "Blessed are they that mourn; for they shall be comforted."—Matt. 5: 4.

Third Pupil. "Blessed are the meek; for they shall inherit the earth."—Matt. 5: 5.

Fourth Pupil. "Blessed are they which do hunger and thirst after righteousness: for they shall be filled."—Matt. 5: 6.

Supt. * "Let us pause here a moment, and invite the skeptic to ascend with us this mount, and look at religion as sketched by the finger of Christ—as it lives and breathes in the words of God's Son—and ask him where is the man—where is the book—in what place, in what age are they to be found—whose words breathe a more divine spirit, and are calculated to form a character more God-like and sublime?"

Supt. CLASS B may now continue the recital of the blessings promised at this time.

First Pupil. "Blessed are the merciful: for they shall obtain mercy."—Matt. 5: 7.

Second Pupil. "Blessed are the pure in heart: for they shall see God."—Matt. 5: 8.

Third Pupil. "Blessed are the peacemakers; for they shall be called the children of God."—Matt. 5: 9.

Fourth Pupil. "Blessed are they which are persecuted for righteousness' sake: for theirs is the kingdom of heaven."—
—Matt. 5: 10.

* "Glimpses of Jesus," Balfern.

Fifth Pupil. "Blessed are ye, when men shall revile you, and persecute you, and shall say all manner of evil against you falsely, for my sake. Rejoice, and be exceeding glad: for great is your reward in heaven: for so persecuted they the prophets which were before you."—Matt. 5: 11, 12.

Singing. Solo and chorus—"The Beatitudes."—Fresh Laurels, p. 136.

Supt. At what time did Christ utter these words?

Teacher. At the beginning of his public ministry, in his sermon on the mount.

Supt. Will CLASS C repeat some of the admonitions given by Christ in this sermon?

First Pupil. "Let your light so shine before men, that they may see your good works, and glorify your Father which is in heaven."—Matt. 5: 16.

Second Pupil. "But I say unto you, That ye resist not evil: but whosoever shall smite thee on thy right cheek, turn to him the other also."—Matt. 5: 39.

Third Pupil. "Give to him that asketh thee, and from him that would borrow of thee turn not thou away."—Matt. 5: 42.

Fourth Pupil. "But I say unto you, Love your enemies, bless them that curse you, do good to them that hate you, and pray for them which despitefully use you, and persecute you."—Matt. 5: 44.

Fifth Pupil. "Be ye therefore perfect, even as your Father which is in heaven is perfect."—Matt. 5: 48.

Supt. CLASS D may remind us of other directions given by him at this time.

First Pupil. "Take heed that ye do not your alms before men, to be seen of them: otherwise ye have no reward of your Father which is in heaven."—Matt. 6: 1.

Second Pupil. "Therefore when thou doest thine alms, do not sound a trumpet before thee, as the hypocrites do in the synagogues and in the streets, that they may have glory of men. Verily I say unto you, they have their reward."—Matt. 6: 2.

Third Pupil. "But when thou doest alms, let not thy left hand know what thy right hand doeth: that thine alms may be in secret: and thy Father which seeth in secret himself shall reward thee openly."—Matt. 6: 3, 4.

Fourth Pupil. "Judge not, that ye be not judged. For with what judgment ye judge, ye shall be judged: and with what measure ye mete, it shall be measured to you again."—Matt. 7: 1, 2.

RECITATION.

Do not look for wrong or evil,
 You will find them if you do;
As you measure to your neighbor,
 He will measure back to you.
Look for goodness, look for gladness;
 You will meet them all the while:
If you bring a smiling visage
 To the glass, you meet a smile.

Supt. Will some member of CLASS E tell us what our Saviour says about accumulating wealth?

First Pupil. "Lay not up for yourselves treasures upon earth, where moth and rust doth corrupt, and where thieves break through and steal: but lay up for yourselves treasures in heaven, where neither moth nor rust doth corrupt, and where thieves do not break through nor steal."—Matt. 6: 19, 20.

Supt. Why cannot we do both?

Second Pupil. "For where your treasure is, there will your heart be also."—Matt. 6: 21.

Third Pupil. "The light of the body is the eye: if therefore thine eye be single, thy whole body shall be full of light."—Matt. 6: 22.

Fourth Pupil. "But if thine eye be evil, thy whole body shall be full of darkness. If therefore the light that is in thee be darkness, how great is that darkness!"—Matt. 6: 23.

Fifth Pupil. "No man can serve two masters: for either he will hate the one and love the other; or else he will hold to the one and despise the other. Ye cannot serve God and mammon."—Matt. 6. 24.

Supt. The whole school may tell me what general rule Christ has given us to regulate our conduct towards each other.

School in Concert. "Therefore all things whatsoever ye would that men should do to you, do ye even so to them."—Matt. 7: 12.

Singing. "The Golden Rule."—Fresh Laurels, p. 28.

Supt. How does Jesus exhort us to exercise a forgiving spirit?

CLASS F.

First Pupil. "For if ye forgive men their trespasses, your heavenly Father will also forgive you."—Matt. 6: 14.

Second Pupil. "But if ye forgive not men their trespasses, neither will your Father forgive your trespasses."—Matt. 6: 15.

Supt. How does he show us what is the highest good and end of life?

CLASS G.

First Pupil. "Therefore I say unto you, Take no thought for your life, what ye shall eat, or what ye shall drink; nor yet for your body, what ye shall put on. Is not the life more than meat, and the body than raiment?"—Matt. 6: 25.

Second Pupil. "Behold the fowls of the air: for they sow not, neither do they reap, nor gather into barns; yet your heavenly Father feedeth them. Are ye not much better than they?"—Matt. 6: 26.

Third Pupil. "And why take ye thought for raiment? Consider the lilies of the field, how they grow; they toil not, neither do they spin: and yet I say unto you, That even Solomon in all his glory was not arrayed like one of these."—Matt. 6: 28, 29.

Fourth Pupil. "Wherefore, if God so clothe the grass of the field, which to-day is, and to-morrow is cast into the oven, shall he not much more clothe you, O ye of little faith?"—Matt. 6: 30.

Fifth Pupil. "Therefore take no thought, saying, What shall we eat? or, What shall we drink? or, Wherewithal shall we be clothed? (for after all these things do the Gentiles seek) for your heavenly Father knoweth that ye have need of all these things."—Matt. 6: 31, 32.

Sixth Pupil. "But seek ye first the kingdom of God, and his righteousness; and all these things shall be added unto you."—Matt. 6: 33.

Supt. CLASS H may repeat in concert Christ's blessed assurance to all who feel their need of him.

"Ask, and it shall be given you; seek, and ye shall find; knock, and it shall be opened unto you: for every one that asketh receiveth; and he that seeketh findeth; and to him that knocketh it shall be opened."—Matt. 7: 7, 8.

Supt. How does he describe the two roads leading to life and death?

Teacher. "Enter ye in at the strait gate: for wide is the gate, and broad is the way, that leadeth to destruction, and many there be which go in thereat: because strait is the gate, and narrow is the way, which leadeth unto life, and few there be that find it."—Matt. 7: 13, 14.

Supt. In what words does he caution us about choosing our guides?

CLASS I.

First Pupil. "Beware of false prophets, which come to you in sheep's clothing, but inwardly they are ravening wolves."—Matt. 7: 15.

Second Pupil. "Ye shall know them by their fruits. Do men gather grapes of thorns, or figs of thistles?"—Matt. 7: 16.

Third Pupil. "Even so every good tree bringeth forth good fruit; but a corrupt tree bringeth forth evil fruit."—Matt. 7: 17.

Fourth Pupil. "A good tree cannot bring forth evil fruit, neither can a corrupt tree bring forth good fruit."—Matt. 7: 18.

Fifth Pupil. "Every tree that bringeth not forth good fruit is hewn down, and cast into the fire. Wherefore by their fruits ye shall know them."—Matt. 7: 19, 20.

Singing. "Prayer for Guidance."—Fresh Laurels, p. 42.

Supt. Does he in this sermon say that any will be left out of his kingdom?

CLASS J.

First Pupil. "Not every one that saith unto me, Lord, Lord, shall enter into the kingdom of heaven; but he that doeth the will of my Father which is in heaven."—Matt. 7: 21.

Second Pupil. "Many will say to me in that day, Lord, Lord, have we not prophesied in thy name? and in thy name have cast out devils? and in thy name done many wonderful works?"—Matt. 7: 22.

Third Pupil. "And then will I profess unto them, I never knew you: depart from me, ye that work iniquity."—Matt. 7: 23.

Supt. How did he illustrate wisdom and folly?

CLASS K.

First Pupil. "Therefore whosoever heareth these sayings of mine, and doeth them, I will liken him unto a wise man, which built his house upon a rock."—Matt. 7: 24.

Second Pupil. "And the rain descended, and the floods came, and the winds blew, and beat upon that house; and it fell not: for it was founded upon a rock."—Matt. 7: 25.

Third Pupil. "And every one that heareth these sayings of mine, and doeth them not, shall be likened unto a foolish man, which built his house upon the sand."—Matt. 7: 26.

Fourth Pupil. "And the rain descended, and the floods came, and the winds blew, and beat upon that house; and it fell: and great was the fall of it."—Matt. 7: 27.

Supt. How did these teachings affect the people?

CLASS L.

First Pupil. "And it came to pass, when Jesus had ended these sayings, the people were astonished at his doctrine."—Matt. 7: 28.

Supt. What caused them to wonder?

Second Pupil. "For he taught them as one having authority, and not as the scribes."—Matt. 7: 29.

Supt. What was the testimony of the officers whom the chief priests and Pharisees sent to take Jesus?

Third Pupil. "Never man spake like this man."—John 7: 46.

Supt. Why have his words and deeds been thus recorded and preserved?

Fourth Pupil. "These are written, that ye might believe that Jesus is the Christ, the son of God; and that believing ye might have life through his name."—John 20: 31.

BRIEF PRAYER BY THE PASTOR.

The Choir responds with the short chant: "Come unto me." (*See Appendix.*)

THE DOXOLOGY.

XI.

Around Gennesaret:

A LESSON FROM THE LIFE OF CHRIST.

"And Jesus went about all the cities and villages, teaching in their synagogues, and preaching the gospel of the kingdom, and healing every sickness and every disease among the people."—*Matt.* 9: 35.

"But straightway Jesus spake unto them, saying, Be of good cheer; it is I; be not afraid."—*Matt.* 14: 27.

EXERCISE.

Opening Chant. "God be merciful unto us and bless us." (*See Appendix.*)

PRAYER.

Singing.

Come every pious heart,
  That loves the Saviour's name,
Your noblest powers exert,
  To celebrate his fame;
* * * * *

Scripture Reading. The 72d Psalm, beginning at the 6th verse. Superintendent and School responsive—

Sing. "Joy to the world, the Lord is come!"

INTRODUCTION.

Superintendent. We are met together to-night for a quiet ramble on the shores of Lake Gennesaret. But before we look upon it with the eyes of the traveler of to-day, let us see Gennesaret as the disciples saw it, and its shores as they were when Jesus walked there 1800 years ago. Could we have stood on Mt. Hatten when Christ delivered his Sermon on the Mount, we should have looked down upon some of the most luxurious vegetation in the world, and upon a lovely lake nestled among the hills three or four miles away. Upon this little strip of water, not thirteen miles long, and in its widest part not seven miles broad, we should have seen vessels going to and fro between the many populous and thriving cities lying on its shores; and beyond the walls of the cities the magnificent temples and synagogues of the Jews dedicated to that God who, when he came among them, they despised. Here was Tiberias, Magdala, Dalmanutha, Chorazin, Capernaum, Gergesa and Gamala, and Josephus tells us of still many more cities containing not less than 15,000 inhabitants. "The public life of Jesus may be said to have had its centre and chief development around the Sea of Galilee. Except the few closing weeks of his life in Jerusalem, the Sea of Galilee witnessed the chief part of his ministrations. Only against the cities on the shores of the lake did he utter maledictions for their obduracy. Upon them he bestowed a long-continued and fruitful activity without a parallel." He mingled with the inhabitants in their daily toil; he taught them in their synagogues; he spoke to them on the shores of the lake, and gathered them around him in the mountains; and even there his audiences numbered thousands from these numerous cities.

We would learn to-night of the mighty works which Christ did here; of the words he spake, and of the fate which befell these cities of Galilee, for here began that organization which has spread over the earth and revolutionized the world. Viewed in this relation, is there a spot on earth that can rival this in interest?

RECITATION.

A Teacher.

1 Blest land of Judea! thrice hallowed of song,
Where the holiest of memories pilgrim-like throng;
In the shade of the palms, by the shores of thy sea,
On the hills of thy beauty, my heart is with thee.

2 Blue sea of the hills! in my spirit I hear
Thy waters, Gennesaret, chime on my ear;
Where the Lowly and Just with the people sat down,
And the spray on the dust of his sandals was thrown.

3 Beyond are Bethulia's mountains of green,
And the desolate hills of the wild Gadarene;
And I pause on the goat-crags of Tabor to see
The gleam of thy waters, O dark Galilee! *Whittier.*

Singing. "Jesus is King."— New Golden Shower, p. 76.

He who once to earth came down,
Toiled and suffered here below,
Sits upon his heavenly throne,
Wears the crown of glory now,
While angels join to sing,
* * * * * *

Supt. We will now hear from the classes concerning some of the incidents of Christ's life; especially his miracles at those cities around Gennesaret.

Class A.

First Pupil. Tiberias was the only city of this region into which Christ never entered, and Magdala is a wretched hamlet of a dozen low huts. This is the city of Mary Magdalene, out of whom were cast seven devils.

(Note.—*The large map must be used in this lesson.*)

Second Pupil. At Gergesa Christ met two possessed with devils, and he cast them out, and they entered a herd of swine, and the whole herd ran down a steep place into the sea.

Third Pupil. "And they that kept them fled, and went their ways into the city, and told everything, and what was befallen to the possessed of the devils. And behold, the whole city came out to meet Jesus; and when they saw him, they besought him that he would depart out of their coasts."— Matt. 8: 33, 34.

Fourth Pupil. Chorazin is mentioned only in Christ's denunciation of the cities wherein he had done mighty works.

Fifth Pupil. "Then began he to upbraid the cities wherein most of his mighty works were done, because they repented not: Woe unto thee, Chorazin! woe unto thee, Bethsaida! for if the mighty works which were done in you, had been done in Tyre and Sidon, they would have repented long ago in sackcloth and ashes."—Matt. 11: 20, 21.

Supt. And what of those cities now?

Teacher. Woe *has* come upon them. The shapeless heaps of Chorazin and Bethsaida "attest impressively the fulfillment of that prophetic curse of the Son of God." So utter and complete their ruin that the traveler of to-day seeks in vain for assurance that he looks upon the site of those once proud cities.

Supt. CLASS B will tell more about Bethsaida.

First Pupil. Bethsaida was the native place of Andrew, Peter and Philip; and here Christ fed the multitude with the five loaves and two fishes.

Second Pupil. Here Mark tells us — 8th chapter, 22d verse — that they brought a blind man unto Christ, and he was restored and saw every man clearly.

Third Pupil. It was nigh unto Bethsaida that the disciples, being in a frail ship on the dark stormy sea, and in great danger, saw "Jesus walking on the sea, and drawing nigh unto the ship: and they were afraid. But he saith unto them, It is I: be not afraid. Then they willingly received him into the ship: and immediately the ship was at the land whither they went." —John 6: 19–21.

Supt. This world is a place of storm and tempest, and on this account it has been compared to the sea. We may learn many lessons of encouragement from this miracle of the Saviour's walking on the stormy sea to his troubled disciples.

We will listen to what the teachers have to say.

A Teacher. We may learn from this miracle, "*that while engaged in doing the will of Christ, storms may overtake us.* 'Many are the storms which blow upon God's trees,' says an old writer, 'to keep them from becoming *earth-bound*.'" *

Another. "*That storms often prepare the way for Jesus to visit his people, with glory to himself and permanent profit to them.* The cause of their trouble is beneath his feet."

* "Glimpses of Jesus," Balfern.

Another. "*That when Jesus comes to his disciples, he comes at the* RIGHT TIME. It is the *seasonableness* of divine mercy which makes it sweet."

Another. "*Also that believers often fear the approach of their greatest mercies.* The storm which frightened the disciples only brought Jesus to their help."

Another. "*That Jesus will travel to the extremity of his people's misery, and save them.* The storm was severe, but it did not keep Christ from the vessel."

Another. "*That apart from Christ, his people can do nothing!*"

1 O cling not, trembler, to life's fragile bark;
It fills — it soon must sink!
Look not below, where all is chill and dark;
'Tis agony to think
Of the wild waste. But look, Oh look above,
And see the outstretched arms of love.
* * * * * *

2 Into his hands commit thy trembling spirit,
Who gave his life for thine.
Guilty, fix all thy trust upon his merit;
To him thy heart resign.
Oh give him love for love, and sweetly fall
Into his hands who is thy all.

Chant. The invitation —"Come Unto Me."
(*See Appendix.*)

Read selection, "The Sea of Galilee," or omit, according to amount of time. (*See Appendix.*)

Supt. Capernaum is called the "Lord's city," for the reason that he spent so much of his mature life here.

CLASS C will give some incidents of the Saviour's life, connected with this city.

First Pupil. While at Cana, a nobleman from Capernaum came and said unto him, "Sir, come down ere my child die. Jesus saith unto him, Go thy way; thy son liveth. And the man believed the word that Jesus had spoken unto him, and he went his way. And as he was now going down, his servants met him, and told him, saying, Thy son liveth."—John 4: 49–51.

Second Pupil. It was near Capernaum that Simon, at the word of the Lord, took the miraculous draught of fishes, recorded in the 5th of Luke.

Third Pupil. An account of Christ's first sabbath at Capernaum is recorded in Luke, 4th chapter — the occasion on which the unclean spirit which he cast out cried out, saying, Let us alone; what have we to do with thee, thou Jesus of Nazareth? art thou come to destroy us? I know thee who thou art; the Holy One of God.

Fourth Pupil. "And he arose out of the synagogue, and entered into Simon's house. And Simon's wife's mother was taken with a great fever, and they besought him for her. And he stood over her, and rebuked the fever; and it left her: and immediately she arose and ministered unto them." — Luke 4: 38, 39.

Fifth Pupil. "And behold, there came a leper and worshiped him, saying, Lord, if thou wilt, thou canst make me clean. And Jesus put forth his hand, and touched him, saying, I will; be thou clean. And immediately his leprosy was cleansed." — Matt. 8: 2, 3.

Singing. "Jesus by the Sea." — Silver Spray, p. 8.

Supt. CLASS D will tell us more about the miracles of Christ.

First Pupil. "And when Jesus was entered into Capernaum, there came unto him a centurion, beseeching him. And saying, Lord, my servant lieth at home sick of the palsy, grievously tormented. And Jesus saith unto him, I will come and heal him." — Matt. 8: 5–7.

Second Pupil. "The centurion answered and said, Lord, I am not worthy that thou shouldst come under my roof: but speak the word only, and my servant shall be healed. And Jesus said unto the centurion, Go thy way; and as thou hast believed, so be it done unto thee. And his servant was healed in the self-same hour." — Matt. 8: 8, 13.

Third Pupil. "And behold, a woman, which was diseased with an issue of blood twelve years, came behind him, and touched the hem of his garment: for she said within herself, If I may but touch his garment, I shall be whole." — Matt. 9: 20, 21.

Fourth Pupil. "But Jesus turned him about, and when he saw her, he said, Daughter, be of good comfort; thy faith hath made thee whole. And the woman was made whole from that hour."—Matt. 9: 22.

Supt. These are only a few of Christ's miracles. They were characterized by love and compassion for the poor and the suffering.

"Then Jesus answering, said unto them, Go your way, and tell John what things ye have seen and heard; how that the blind see, the lame walk, the lepers are cleansed, the deaf hear, the dead are raised, to the poor the gospel is preached. And blessed is he, whosoever shall not be offended in me."—Luke 7: 22, 23.

Asst. Supt. "And there are also many other things which Jesus did, the which, if they should be written every one, I suppose that even the world itself could not contain the books that should be written. Amen."—John 21: 25.

A Teacher.

How beauteous on the mountains are thy feet,
Thy form how comely, and thy voice how sweet,
Son of the Highest! Who can tell thy fame?
The deaf shall hear it, while the dumb proclaim!
Now bid the blind behold their Saviour's light,
The lame go forth rejoicing in their might;
Cleanse with a touch yon kneeling leper's skin,
Cheer this pale penitent, forgive her sin;
Oh! for that mother's faith, her daughter spare;
Restore the maniac to a father's prayer;
Pity the tears those mourning sisters shed,
And be *the resurrection of the dead.*

Singing. "Happy Voices," p. 27.

I think, when I read that sweet story of old,
When Jesus was here among men.

Superintendent Closing.

How strikingly the course of nature tells,
By its light heed of human suffering,
That it was fashioned for a happier world.
*   *   *   *   *   *   *

The traveler to-day looks out upon the sparkling waters of Lake Gennesaret, in their bright emerald setting, and, save the beauty of the scene, finds naught of interest to the outward eye. The smiling face of nature gives no sign that upon these shores has been fulfilled the fearful denunciation of Christ. "O sea, what changes hast thou seen!" The cities' thronging streets, the thousands of care-encumbered men who trod the shores have passed away, and now here rests "the stillness of central sea."

Tiberias yet exists; but the long belt of proud and busy homes that encompassed this inland lake is gone, and men from distant lands grope among the thorns or overgrown heaps of stone, disputing the position of one and another city which, in the days of Jesus, seemed too strong to be ever wasted. Both around the sea, and in all the country far away on each side of it, the cities and homes have utterly perished. Temples and synagogues are gone. Walls of towns and marble palaces are in heaps. The architectural ambition of Herod, the city-building aspirations of the Greeks, the engineering achievements of the Romans, all alike have hopelessly perished. The Lake of Gennesaret is without a boat. Its fish swarm unmolested. The soil adjacent runs rankly to thorns and briers; only a few Arabs hover about its edges. But one thing remains: it is the memory of Jesus. The sky, the surrounding hills and the water have one story to tell the educated traveler. Jesus still wanders slowly along these deserted shores. His spirit yet walks upon these waters, and the very name of this plain and solitary lake sends a thrill to the heart of every one who hears it.

1 And what if my feet may not tread where he stood,
Nor my ears hear the dashing of Galilee's flood,
Nor my eyes see the cross which he bowed him to bear,
Nor my knees press Gethsemane's garden of prayer.

2 Yet, loved of thy Father, thy spirit is near
To the meek and the lowly and penitent here;
And the voice of thy love is the same even now
As at Bethany's tomb or on Olivet's brow.

3 Oh, the outward hath gone! — but, in glory and power,
The spirit surviveth the things of an hour;
Unchanged, undecaying, its Pentecost flame,
On the heart's secret altar is burning the same!

Whittier.

Closing Song. "Looking to Jesus."— Notes of Joy, p. 127.

XII.

Christ the Foundation Stone:

A LESSON CONCERNING THE "LIVING STONES" IN "GOD'S BUILDING."

"The stone which the builders rejected, the same is become the head of the corner."—*Matt.* 21: 42.

"Ye also as lively stones, are built up a spiritual house, a holy priesthood, to offer up spiritual sacrifices, acceptable to God by Jesus Christ."—1 *Pet.* 2: 5.

EXERCISE.

Chant. The 95th Psalm.

Oh, come, let us sing unto the Lord;
Let us heartily rejoice in the strength of our salvation.

(*See Appendix.*)

Scripture Reading. By the Superintendent — 1 Peter 2: 1–9. Also, Superintendent and School read or repeat in concert, the "Apostles' Creed."

(*See Appendix.*)

School Chant. "The Lord's Prayer."

(*See Appendix.*)

The Choir chant the "Gloria Patri."

(*See Appendix.*)

Singing. "Beautiful Land" (or substitute). — Happy Voices, p. 193.

1 Jerusalem, for ever bright,
Beautiful land of rest;
No winter there, nor chill of night—
Beautiful land of rest.
The dripping cloud is chased away,
The sun breaks forth in endless day:
Jerusalem,
The beautiful land of rest!

CHORUS.—We wait impatient to behold
The gates of pearl, the streets of gold,
And nestle safe in Jesus' fold,
In the beautiful land,
The beautiful land of rest!

2 Jerusalem, for ever free,
Beautiful land of rest,
The soul's sweet home of liberty,
Beautiful land of rest!
The gyves of sin, the chains of woe,
The ransomed there will never know.
Jerusalem,
The beautiful land of rest!

CHORUS.

3 Jerusalem, for ever dear,
Beautiful land of rest,
Thy pearly gates almost appear,
Beautiful land of rest!
And when we tread thy lovely shore,
We'll sing the song we've sung before,
Jerusalem,
The beautiful land of rest!

CHORUS.

Recitation or Song by a class from the infant department.

THE LESSON.

Superintendent. What is contained in the books of Moses about the rock?

Teacher. "Behold, I will stand before thee there upon the rock in Horeb; and thou shalt smite the rock, and there shall come water out of it, that the people may drink."—Ex. 17: 6.

First Pupil. "And Moses lifted up his hand, and with his rod he smote the rock twice, and the water came out abundantly, and the congregation drank, and their beasts also."—Num. 20: 11.

Second Pupil. "He is the rock, his work is perfect, for all his ways are judgment; a God of truth, and without iniquity, just and right is he."—Deut. 32: 4.

Supt. What did the prophets Isaiah and Zechariah say?

Teacher. "Because thou hast forgotten the God of thy salvation, and hast not been mindful of the Rock of thy strength, therefore shalt thou plant pleasant plants, and shalt set it with strange slips, * * * but the harvest shall be a heap in the day of grief and of desperate sorrow."—Is. 17: 10, 11.

Third Pupil. "Behold a king shall reign in righteousness, and princes shall rule in judgment. And a man shall be as an hiding-place from the wind, and a covert from the tempest, as rivers of water in a dry place, as the shadow of a great rock in a weary land."—Is. 32: 1, 2.

Fourth Pupil. "Therefore, thus saith the Lord God, Behold I lay in Zion for a foundation a stone, a tried stone, a precious corner stone, a sure foundation; he that believeth shall not make haste."—Is. 28: 16.

Fifth Pupil. "Who art thou, O great mountain? Before Zerubbabel thou shall become a plain, and he shall bring forth the headstone thereof with shoutings, crying Grace, grace unto it."—Zech. 4: 7.

Supt. What was Daniel's prophecy?

Teacher. "Thou sawest till that a stone was cut out without hands, which smote the image upon his feet that were of iron and clay, and brake them to pieces."—Dan. 2: 34.

Sixth Pupil. "Then was the iron, the clay, the brass, the silver, and the gold broken to pieces together, and became like the chaff of the summer threshing floors; and the wind carried them away, that no place was found for them; and the stone that smote the image became a great mountain, and filled the whole earth."—Dan. 2: 35.

Supt. What did Christ say about the foundation-stone?

Teacher. "Therefore whosoever heareth these sayings of mine and doeth them, I will liken him unto a wise man, which built his house upon a rock."—Matt. 7: 24.

Seventh Pupil. "And the rain descended, and the floods came, and the winds blew, and beat upon that house, and it fell not, for it was founded upon a rock."—Matt. 7: 25.

Eighth Pupil. "And I say also unto thee that thou art Peter, and upon this rock I will build my church, and the gates of hell shall not prevail against it."—Matt. 16: 18.

Ninth Pupil. "Jesus saith unto them, Did ye never read in the Scriptures, The stone which the builders rejected, the same is become the head of the corner. This is the Lord's doing, and it is marvelous in our eyes?"—Matt. 21: 42.

Supt. What did Peter say about the living stone?

Teacher. "To whom coming as unto a living stone, disallowed indeed of men, but chosen of God, and precious."—1 Pet. 2: 4.

Tenth Pupil. "Ye, also, as lively stones, are built up a spiritual house, a holy priesthood, to offer up spiritual sacrifices acceptable to God by Jesus Christ."—1 Peter 2: 5.

Eleventh Pupil. "Wherefore, also, it is contained in the Scripture, Behold I lay in Zion a chief corner-stone, elect, precious; and he that believeth on him shall not be confounded."—1 Peter 2: 6.

Twelfth Pupil. "Unto you therefore which believe he is precious; but unto them which be disobedient, the stone which the builders disallowed, the same is made the head of the corner."—1 Peter 2: 7.

Supt. What was Paul's testimony about the rock?

Teacher. "Now, therefore, ye are no more strangers and foreigners, but fellow-citizens with the saints, and of the household of God; and are built upon the foundation of the apostles and prophets, Jesus Christ himself being the chief corner-stone."—Eph. 2: 19, 20.

Thirteenth Pupil. "Moreover, brethren, I would not that ye should be ignorant, how that all our fathers were under the cloud, and all passed through the sea: and were all baptized unto Moses in the cloud and in the sea."—1 Cor. 10: 1, 2.

Fourteenth Pupil. "And did all eat the same spiritual meat; and did all drink the same spiritual drink; for they drank of that spiritual Rock that followed them, and that Rock was Christ."—1 Cor. 10: 3, 4.

Member of Bible Class.

Drink, weary pilgrim, if athirst thou be,
Know that the stream is gushing forth for thee;
Drink in Christ's name—life's painful way who trod,
Man gives the cup—the living water, God.

Singing. "The Water of Life."—Fresh Laurels, p. 50.

Supt. What did John, the Revelator, behold and describe?

Teacher. "And he carried me away in the spirit to a great and high mountain, and showed me that great city, the holy Jerusalem, descending out of heaven from God, having the glory of God; and her light was like unto a stone most precious, even like a jasper stone, clear as crystal."—Rev. 21: 10, 11.

Fifteenth Pupil. "And the foundations of the walls of the city were garnished with all manner of precious stones. The first foundation was jasper, the second sapphire, the third a chalcedony, the fourth an emerald."—Rev. 21: 19.

Sixteenth Pupil. "The fifth, sardonyx; the sixth, sardius; the seventh, chrysolite; the eighth, beryl; the ninth, a topaz; the tenth, chrysoprasus; the eleventh, a jacinth; the twelfth, an amethyst."—Rev. 21: 20.

Seventeenth Pupil. "He that hath an ear, let him hear what the Spirit saith unto the churches: To him that overcometh will I give to eat of the hidden manna, and will give him a white stone, and in the stone a new name written, which no man knoweth saving he that receiveth it."—Rev. 2: 17.

Member of Ladies' Bible Class.

I want, oh! I want to attain
  Some likeness, my Saviour, to thee;
That longed-for resemblance once more to regain,
  Thy comeliness put upon me—
I want to be marked for thy own;
  Thy seal on my forehead to wear;
To receive that "new name" on the mystic white stone,
  Which only thyself canst declare.

— *Changed Cross.*

Supt. What are the words of the Psalmist?

Teacher. "Behold he smote the rock, that the waters gushed out, and the streams overflowed."—Ps. 78: 20.

Eighteenth Pupil. "He only is my rock and my salvation; he is my defence; I shall not be greatly moved."—Ps. 62: 2.

Nineteenth Pupil. "For in the time of trouble he shall hide me in his pavilion; in the secret of his tabernacle shall he hide me; he shall set me up upon a rock."—Ps. 27: 5.

Twentieth Pupil. "From the end of the earth will I cry unto thee, when my heart is overwhelmed; lead me to the rock that is higher than I. For thou hast been a shelter for me, and a strong tower from the enemy."—Ps. 61: 2, 3.

Member of Bible Class.

When the fierce noon-tide beats upon my head:
When, weary, still I toil for daily bread;
When the dark storm-clouds gather o'er my way,
Then, my deliverer, be my strength and stay!
I shall not fear the tempest's sudden shock,
If sheltered 'neath the everlasting rock.

Teacher. "Bow down thine ear to me; deliver me speedily; be thou my strong rock, for an house of defence, to save me."—31: 2.

Twenty-first Pupil. "To show that the Lord is upright; he is my rock, and there is no unrighteousness in him."—Ps. 92: 15.

Twenty-second Pupil. "He brought me up also out of a horrible pit, out of the miry clay, and set my feet upon a rock, and established my goings."—Ps. 40: 2.

Twenty-third Pupil. "Be thou my strong habitation, whereunto I may continually resort; thou hast given commandment to save me, for thou art my rock and my fortress."—Ps. 71: 3.

Twenty-fourth Pupil. "He shall cry unto me, Thou art my father, my God, and the rock of my salvation."—Ps. 89: 26.

Twenty-fifth Pupil. "The Lord is my rock, and my fortress, and my deliverer; my God, my strength, in whom I will trust; my buckler, and the hour of my salvation, and my high tower."—Ps. 18: 2.

Asst. Supt. "O my dove, that art in the clefts of the rock, in the secret places of the stairs, let me see thy countenance, let me hear thy voice, for sweet is thy voice, and thy countenance is comely."—Song of Solomon 2: 14.

A Lady Teacher.

"My dove!" the bridegroom speaks. To whom?
Whom, think'st thou, meaneth he?
Say, O my soul! canst thou presume
He thus addresseth thee?
Yes, 'tis the bridegroom's voice of love,
Calling thee, O my soul, his dove!

Another.

My soul, of native power bereft,
  To calvary repairs;
Immanuel is the *rocky cleft*,
  The secret of the stairs!
Since placed *there* by the bridegroom's love,
What evil can befall his dove?

Another.

My soul, now hid within a rock,
  (The "Rock of Ages" called,)
Amid the universal shock,
  Is fearless, unappalled.
A cleft therein, prepared by love,
In safety hides the bridegroom's dove.

Another.

O thou, who on the bridegroom's head
  Didst as a dove come down,
Within my soul thy graces shed,
  Establish there thy throne;
There shed abroad a Saviour's love,
Thou holy, pure, and heavenly dove!

— *Changed Cross.*

Singing. "Rock of Ages."

The following extract* may be read, or the substance of it given in remarks by pastor or superintendent:

LIVING STONES.

"Ye are God's building."—1 Cor. 3: 9.

"For many centuries the problem was unsolved as to the sources whence the stones used in the substructions of Solomon's temple were procured. But it is now known that Jerusalem, like Rome, has yawning beneath it extensive catacombs, or subterranean excavations, whence vast quantities of pure white stone have been taken in ages past.

"A traveler, after having explored these dark caverns, says:

"'For some time we were almost overcome with awe and admiration. At first there was a constant descent, till we had proceeded about a thousand feet from the entrance. Rude natural pillars, as in modern mines, had been left by the

* From a sermon by Rev. E. C. Anderson, Portland, Oregon.

ancient workmen to prevent the roof from crushing in. Here the darkness was most intense, and the echoes of our footsteps and voices almost startling. Now, from the floor of this cave there is a gently inclined plane all the way to the site of the temple, and this may easily solve the problem as to the transportation of those immense blocks in its foundations.'

"The building of the earthly temple shall teach us a lesson of God's spiritual building.

"The contrast between this dark quarry and the sunny summit of the temple mount was not more marked than is the condition of sin and sorrow in which the Saviour finds us, compared with the glory unto which he will bring us.

"Even the highest knowledge attainable here, like the light cast by the workmen in this cave, is feeble and partial compared with the light of heavenly day. For though we have, in the word of God, a 'light to our feet and a lamp to our path,' yet impenetrable shadows project themselves all around us.

"The present life is in like manner the scene of fitting and fashioning the living stones for their places in glory.

"Every living stone, when translated out of this darkness to that marvelous light, will be more transfigured than were the stones of that cavern when transferred to the radiant walls of the temple. And their gratitude and bliss will rise higher as they look back to the rock from whence they were hewn, and to the hole of the pit whence they were digged.

"How vividly do these heaps of chips and fragments, strewing its floor, remind us of the imperfections, failings, and besetting sins of the living stones, who left them all behind, as they were borne forth to the realm of heavenly day. And what were the drills, wedges, hammers, and chisels, whose sounds were so constantly echoing in those dark recesses, but indices pointing, with significant fingers, to the sharp processes of trial and sorrow, whereof all are partakers who are the acknowledged children of God.

"But when they are borne to their niches in the temple above, they will see, amid the light of that brighter day, that none of these painful strokes could have been kindly or wisely spared; that they were all directed by a wisdom that could not and a love that would not mistake. The last tear will then be wiped away in gladness; the last muttered complaint will rise into praise; the last sigh will swell into new songs; and death itself will be swallowed up in victory.

"The terms *Zion* and *Jerusalem* are now more readily suggestive of the delectable mount of heavenly sunshine, of the city of everlasting habitations, than they are of the mount and city to which they were first given. 'For ye are come unto Mount Zion, to the city of the living God, to the heavenly Jerusalem, and to an innumerable company of angels, to the general assembly and church of the first-born, who are enrolled in heaven, and to God the judge of all, and to the spirits of the just ones made perfect.'"

Oh when, thou city of my God,
Shall I thy courts ascend?
Blest seats, through rude and stormy scenes,
We onward press to you.

Closing Song. "Beautiful Zion."—Happy Voices, p. 213.

XIII.

The Name of Jesus:

A LESSON FROM THE TITLES OF CHRIST.

"The name of the Lord is a strong tower: the righteous runneth into it and is safe."—*Prov.* 18: 10.

"And his name shall be called Wonderful, Counsellor, The Mighty God, The Everlasting Father, The Prince of Peace."—*Is.* 9: 6.

EXERCISE.

By Superintendent and School. The Lord's Prayer, in concert.

(*Repeat slowly and distinctly—every voice.*)

Singing. "The Children's Te Deum" (or substitute).—Fresh Laurels, p. 104.

We praise thee, we bless thee! Thou who only art divine,
No name is worthy such homage as thine;
Our hearts' adoration forever we will gladly bring
To thee, our Redeemer, Creator, and King.

Scripture Reading. Superintendent and School, responsively, the 145th Psalm.

Supt. "I will extol thee, my God, O King; and I will bless thy name for ever and ever."

School. "Every day will I bless thee; and I will praise thy name for ever and ever."

(*To the end of the chapter—or the 8th Psalm.*)

Singing. "Autumn."—Fresh Laurels, p. 59.

1 Hail, my ever-blessed Jesus,
Only thee I wish to sing;
To my soul thy name is precious,
Thou my Prophet, Priest, and King.
Oh what mercy flows from heaven!
Oh what joy and happiness!
Love I much? I'm much forgiven,
I'm a miracle of grace.

2 Shout, ye bright angelic choir,
Praise the Lamb enthroned above:
While astonished, I admire
God's free grace and boundless love.
That blest moment I received him,
Filled my soul with joy and peace.
Love I much? I'm much forgiven,
I'm a miracle of grace.

RECITATION.

(*Make selection from Appendix.*)

Supt. The name of Jesus.

"Wherefore God also hath highly exalted him, and given him a name which is above every name: that at the name of Jesus every knee should bow, of things in heaven, and things in earth, and things under the earth."—Phil. 2: 9, 10.

A Teacher.

1 How sweet the name of Jesus sounds
In a believer's ear;
It soothes his sorrows, heals his wounds,
And drives away his fear.

2 It makes the wounded spirit whole,
And calms the troubled breast;
'Tis manna to the hungry soul,
And to the weary rest.

3 Jesus, my Shepherd, Guardian, Friend,
My Prophet, Priest, and King.
My Lord, my life, my way, my end,
Accept the praise we bring.

Supt. The titles of Jesus in the prophecies of his coming.

CLASS A.

First Pupil. "The sceptre shall not depart from Judah, nor a law-giver from between his feet, until Shiloh come; and unto him shall the gathering of the people be."—Gen. 49: 10.

Second Pupil. "I shall see him, but not now; I shall behold him, but not nigh; there shall come a Star out of Jacob, and a Sceptre shall rise out of Israel, and shall smite the corners of Moab, and destroy all the children of Sheth."—Num. 24: 17.

Third Pupil. "Therefore the Lord himself shall give you a sign; Behold, a virgin shall conceive, and bear a son, and shall call his name Immanuel."—Is. 7: 14.

Fourth Pupil. "And there shall come forth a rod out of the stem of Jesse, and a Branch shall grow out of his roots."—Is. 11: 1.

Fifth Pupil. "For unto us a child is born, unto us a son is given; and the government shall be upon his shoulder; and his name shall be called Wonderful, Counsellor, The Mighty God, The Everlasting Father, The Prince of Peace."—Is. 9: 6.

Sixth Pupil. "But unto you that fear my name shall the Son of Righteousness arise with healing in his wings; and ye shall go forth, and grow up as calves of the stall."—Mal. 4: 2.

Teacher.

So spake the prophets — to the earth
Proclaiming thus a Saviour's birth.
God called him Jesus, but a nation's need
Gave to the lowly infant, titles more
Than any earthly monarch ever wore.

Supt. What titles show the divinity of Christ?

CLASS B.

First Pupil. "And she shall bring forth a son, and thou shalt call his name Jesus, for he shall save his people from their sins."—Matt. 1: 21.

Second Pupil. "Then they that were in the ship came and worshiped him, saying, Of a truth thou art the Son of God."—Matt. 14: 33.

Third Pupil. "Saying, Let us alone; what have we to do with thee, thou Jesus of Nazareth? Art thou come to destroy us? I know thee who thou art, the Holy One of God."—Mark 1: 24.

Fourth Pupil. "He shall be great, and shall be called the Son of the Highest, and the Lord God shall give unto him the throne of his father David."—Luke 1: 32.

Fifth Pupil. "For unto you is born this day, in the city of David, a Saviour which is Christ the Lord."—Luke 2: 11.

Sixth Pupil. "And Thomas answered and said unto him, My Lord and my God."—John 20: 28.

Supt. What titles show Christ as a sovereign?

CLASS C.

First Pupil. "And Jesus stood before the governor; and the governor asked him, saying, Art thou the King of the Jews? And Jesus said unto him, Thou sayest."—Matt. 27: 11.

Second Pupil. "But ye denied the Holy One and the Just, and desired a murderer to be granted unto you; and killed the Prince of Life, whom God hath raised from the dead; whereof we are witnesses."—Acts 3; 14, 15.

Third Pupil. "And he commanded us to preach unto the people, and to testify that it is he which was ordained of God to be the Judge of quick and dead."—Acts 10: 42.

Fourth Pupil. "My brethren, have not the faith of our Lord Jesus Christ, the Lord of Glory, with respect of persons." —James 2: 1.

Fifth Pupil. "And he hath on his vesture and on his thigh a name written, King of kings and Lord of lords."—Rev. 19: 16.

Supt. What titles show Christ as Mediator?

CLASS B.

First Pupil. "And to Jesus, the mediator of the new covenant, and to the blood of sprinkling, that speaketh better things than that of Abel."—Heb. 12: 24.

Second Pupil. "Seeing then that we have a great High Priest that is passed unto the heavens, Jesus the Son of God, let us hold fast our profession."—Heb. 4: 14.

Third Pupil. "Whither the forerunner is for us entered, even Jesus, made a high priest forever after the order of Melchisedec."—Heb. 6: 20.

Fourth Pupil. "My little children, these things I write unto you, that ye sin not. And if any man sin, we have an Advocate with the Father, Jesus Christ the Righteous."—1 John 2: 1.

Fifth Pupil. "Saying with a loud voice, Worthy is the Lamb that was slain to receive power, and riches, and wisdom, and strength, and honor, and glory, and blessing."—Rev. 5: 12.

Sixth Pupil. "I am the Door; by me if any man enter in, he shall be saved, and shall go in and out and find pasture."—John 10: 9.

RECITATION.

By three children from the INFANT CLASS.

First Child. Little lips may speak his praise,
Tell how great the Son of God.
We have learned to worship too,
Learned to sound his name abroad.

Second Child. Little tongues may sing of Christ,
Tell the wonders he has wrought,
Promises that shall be ours
If we serve him as we ought.

Third Child. Little hearts may throb with love,
For the Saviour, Jesus dear.
We may serve him here on earth,
Live with him forever there.

All. Let us strive with heart and voice,
Busy brain, and busy hand,
Thus to serve him here on earth,
Meet him in the heavenly land.

Singing. "Love for Jesus" (or substitute).—Fresh Laurels, p. 23.

1 I love the name of Jesus,
That name the angels sing;
And with their loud hosannas,
The heavenly portals ring.
To him my all confiding,
In him my joy complete,
I learn with Christian meekness
My duty at his feet.
CHORUS.—I love, I love,
I love the name of Jesus:
The sweetest name, the name,
The name the angels sing.

2 I love to think of Jesus,
When all is calm and still;
When pure and holy feelings
My grateful bosom fill.
I love to think of Jesus,
Whose mercy crowns my days,
How just are all his counsels,
And true are all his ways.
CHORUS.

3 I love to work for Jesus,
  And worship at his throne;
Oh, may his Spirit help me
  To live for him alone.
To labor for my Saviour
  My greatest joy shall be;
I know that Jesus loves me
  Because he died for me.
CHORUS.

Supt. Jesus the way, the truth, and the life.

CLASS E.

First Pupil. "Jesus saith unto him, I am the way, the truth, and the life; no man cometh unto the Father but by me." —John 14: 6.

Teacher. Come my way, my truth, my life,
  Such a way as gives us breath,
Such a truth as ends all strife,
  Such a life as killeth death.

Second Pupil. "Then spake Jesus again unto them, saying, I am the light of the world; he that followeth me, shall not walk in darkness, but shall have the light of life."—John 8: 12.

Third Pupil. "I am the bread of life."—John 6: 35.

Fourth Pupil. "The Lord is their strength, and he is the saving strength of his anointed."— Ps. 28: 8.

Teacher. Come my light, my feast, my strength,
  Such a light as shows a feast,
Such a feast as mends in length,
  Such a strength, as makes his guest.

RECITATION.

By a member of the BIBLE CLASS.

Jesus, no other word so sweet,
In that dear name, all heart-joys meet;
  But sweeter than the honey far,
  The glimpses of his presence are.
No name is heard more sweet than this,
No word is sung so full of bliss,
  No thought brings sweeter comfort nigh,
  Than Jesus, Son of God, most High.

O Jesus! king of wondrous might,
O victor! glorious from the fight,
  Sweetness that cannot be expressed,
  And altogether loveliest.
Jesus, the hope of souls forlorn,
How good to them for sin that mourn,
  To them that seek thee, oh! how kind,
  But what art thou to them that find!
No tongue of mortal can express,
No letters write its blessedness.
  Alone who hath thee in his heart,
  Knows, love of Jesus, what thou art.

Singing. "Jesus lover of my soul."

Supt. What titles show Christ's characteristics?

CLASS F.

First Pupil. "And, behold, there was a man in Jerusalem, whose name was Simeon; and the same man was just and devout, waiting for the consolation of Israel, and the Holy Ghost was upon him."— Luke 2: 25.

Second Pupil. "The Son of Man came eating and drinking, and they say, Behold a gluttonous and a winebibber, a friend of publicans and sinners. But wisdom is justified of her children."— Matt. 11: 19.

Third Pupil. "And looking upon Jesus as he walked, he said, Behold the Lamb of God."— John 1: 36.

Fourth Pupil. "And one of the elders saith unto me: Weep not, behold the Lion of the tribe of Juda, the root of David, hath prevailed to open the book, and to loose the seven seals thereof."— Rev. 5: 5.

Fifth Pupil. "But when Jesus heard that, he said unto them, They that be whole need not a physician, but they that are sick."— Matt. 9: 12.

Sixth Pupil. "And he shall sit as a refiner and purifier of silver, and he shall purify the sons of Levi, and purge them as gold and silver, that they may offer unto the Lord an offering in righteousness."— Mal. 3: 3.

Seventh Pupil. "And did all drink the same spiritual drink: for they drank of that spiritual Rock that followed them, and that Rock was Christ."— 1 Cor. 10: 4.

Superintendent or Pastor. As there is no want in human nature Christ does not meet, so there is no title lacking to show our Saviour as the embodiment of all we can desire. Nearly one hundred titles tell us what Christ can be to man. He is a "covert," a "hiding-place," a "shepherd," and a "leader" to guide us to God, and then a "witness" for us. To a world in darkness, he came as "light," as a "bright and morning star" to guide; as the "sun" to warm and enlighten; yea, even as "the brightness of the Father's glory," he shone upon them. He is an "ensign" for his followers to rally around, and then a "captain" and a "commander" to lead them on to victory. He is a loving "bridegroom," or a gentle "teacher." He is a "vine" to strengthen, a "root" to sustain. He is the "Alpha and Omega," the "author and finisher," the "Amen." He is indeed the "Wonderful.' Look through all history, and in whom do all these attributes exist but in the Redeemer of the world! He alone can be the "hope" of the world: he alone can be the "desire of all nations. Is he our "hope?" Is he our "desire?"

Singing. "All hail the power of Jesus' name."

XIV.

Christ to the Churches:

A LESSON OF WARNING AND OF PROMISE.

"He that hath an ear, let him hear what the Spirit saith unto the churches."

"Blessed is he that readeth, and they that hear the words of this prophecy, and keep those things which are written therein."—Rev. 1 : 3.

EXERCISE.

Opening Song. "The Lord is King."—Notes of Joy, p. 38.

Praise the Lord all ye people,
  Oh, lift up your voice,
Let the floods clap their hands,
  And the mountains rejoice.

CHORUS — We will praise him, we will praise him,
We will join the mighty mighty chorus,
For the Lord is our God,
For the Lord is our King.

PRAYER.

Chant. "God be merciful unto us."—67th Psalm. (*See Appendix.*)

SCRIPTURE READING.

First Asst. Supt. Rev. 1: 1–3.
Second Asst. Supt. Rev. 1: 4–6.
Supt. Rev. 1: 8–11.
Pastor. Rev. 1: 12–13, 17–20.

Singing. Anthem, "Exalt Him all ye people."—Fresh Laurels, 131.

Here give a brief description of the geography of the lesson (using the board or map), the location of the cities of the seven churches and of the Isle of Patmos; also an account of the establishment of these churches, of the banishment of John, of the vision, etc.

Singing. "I love thy kingdom, Lord."

THE CHURCH OF EPHESUS.

CLASS A.

First Pupil. "Unto the angel of the church of Ephesus write: These things saith he that holdeth the seven stars in his right hand, who walketh in the midst of the seven golden candlesticks."

Supt. How does Christ address this church?

Second Pupil. "I know thy works, and thy labor, and thy patience, and how thou canst not bear them which are evil: and thou hast tried them which say they are apostles, and are not, and hast found them liars."

Supt. What does Christ here commend?

Third Pupil. Christ commends their labor for his cause, their patience with sinners, and their refusal of evil. "And hast borne, and hast patience, and for my name's sake hast labored, and hast not fainted."

Fourth Pupil. Christ said to them, "Nevertheless I have somewhat against thee, because thou hast left thy first love."

Fifth Pupil. This means that they had lost the warm, tender love to Jesus and to each other, that they had at the time of their conversion, and this was the warning given: "Remember therefore from whence thou art fallen, and repent, and do the first works; or else I will come unto thee quickly, and will remove thy candlestick out of his place, except thou repent."

Supt. And what is the precious promise to this church?

Sixth Pupil. "He that hath an ear, let him hear what the Spirit saith unto the churches: To him that overcometh will I give to eat of the tree of life, which is in the midst of the paradise of God."

Teacher. 1 Had I such faith in God,
As mountains to remove,
No faith could work effectual good
That did not work by love.

2 Grant, then, this one request—
Whatever be denied—
That love divine may rule my breast,
And all my actions guide.

THE CHURCH OF SMYRNA.

Class B.

First Pupil. "And unto the angel of the church in Smyrna write: These things saith the first and the last, which was dead, and is alive."

Supt. What is the meaning of the title which Christ assumes in this message?

Second Pupil. It means that Christ is the ever-living God, and teaches the lesson of the resurrection from the dead.

"Jesus said unto her, I am the resurrection and the life: he that believeth in me, though he were dead, yet shall he live."—John 11: 25.

Supt. How did this church compare with the others?

Third Pupil. It was the poorest and the purest; and the use of this title of the ever-living, in the Spirit's message to this poor suffering church of martyrs, was to encourage them with the hope of the future life.

Fourth Pupil. "For we know that if our earthly house of this tabernacle were dissolved, we have a building of God, an house not made with hands, eternal in the heavens."—2 Cor. 5: 1.

Supt. What lesson is here taught concerning poverty and riches?

Fifth Pupil. "I know thy works, and tribulation, and poverty, but thou art rich."

"There is that maketh himself rich, yet hath nothing: there is that maketh himself poor, yet hath great riches."—Prov. 13: 7.

Supt. What was the blessed promise to the church at Smyrna?

Sixth Pupil. "Be thou faithful unto death, and I will give thee a crown of life."—Matt. 10: 28.

"He that hath an ear, let him hear what the Spirit saith unto the churches: He that overcometh shall not be hurt of the second death."

Singing. "Jesus, I my cross have taken."

THE CHURCH OF PERGAMOS.

CLASS C.

Supt. How did Jesus announce himself to the church of Pergamos?

First Pupil. "And to the angel of the church in Pergamos write: These things saith he which hath the sharp sword with two edges."

Supt. What is meant by the two-edged sword?

Second Pupil. It means the word of God.

"For the word of God is quick and powerful, and sharper than any two-edged sword, piercing even to the dividing asunder of soul and spirit, and of the joints and marrow, and is a discerner of the thoughts and intents of the heart."— Heb. 4: 12.

Supt. For what is this church commended?

Third Pupil. For faithfulness under persecution.

"I know thy works, and where thou dwellest, even where Satan's seat is: and thou holdest fast my name, and hast not denied my faith, even in those days wherein Antipas was my faithful martyr, who was slain among you, where Satan dwelleth."

Supt. For what was it upbraided?

Fourth Pupil. "But I have a few things against thee, because thou hast there them that hold the doctrine of Balaam, who taught Balak to cast a stumbling-block before the children of Israel, to eat things sacrificed unto idols, and to commit fornication."

Supt. What was the warning given?

Fifth Pupil. "Repent: or else I will come unto thee quickly, and will fight against them with the sword of my mouth."

Supt. What was the Spirit's message to this church?

Sixth Pupil. "To him that overcometh will I give to eat of the hidden manna, and will give him a white stone, and in the stone a new name written, which no man knoweth saving he that receiveth it."

Teacher. Give us the "hidden" grace,
The "manna" from above;
The "white stone" secretly inscribed,
With thy "new name" of love.

RECITATION.

A little girl repeats the following from the platform:

1 What can I do for Jesus,
Who died that I might live?
I have no precious jewels,
No costly gems to give.

2 My hands are weak to labor,
But all my earthly days,
My lips shall tell his story,
My tongue repeat his praise.

3 He is my tender shepherd;
I'll ask him every day,
To guide me to his pastures,
And never let me stray.

Supt. The lesson of the church in Thyatira is in many respects like that of Pergamos. We will now hear concerning

THE CHURCH OF SARDIS.

CLASS D.

Supt. What does Christ say of this church?

First Pupil. "And unto the angel of the church in Sardis write: These things saith he that hath the seven Spirits of God, and the seven stars: I know thy works, that thou hast a name that thou livest, and art dead."

Second Pupil. I have a Bible illustration concerning Christians of this class:

"And that which fell among thorns are they, which when they have heard, go forth, and are choked with cares, and riches, and pleasures of this life, and bring no fruit to perfection."—Luke 8: 14.

Supt. What is the admonition to this church?

Third Pupil. "Be watchful, and strengthen the things which remain, that are ready to die: for I have not found thy works perfect before God."

Fourth Pupil. "Remember therefore how thou hast received and heard, and hold fast, and repent. If therefore thou shalt not watch, I will come on thee as a thief, and thou shalt not know what hour I will come upon thee."

Supt. What words of comfort, and what reward to the faithful?

Fifth Pupil. "Thou hast a few names even in Sardis which have not defiled their garments: and they shall walk with me in white: for they are worthy."

Sixth Pupil. "He that overcometh, the same shall be clothed in white raiment: and I will not blot out his name out of the book of life, but I will confess his name before my Father, and before his angels."

Teacher. Oh may we never be
As "dead" souls in thy sight;
But live that we in heaven may see
And walk with thee in white!

Supt. Dr. Gregory, in his notes upon this lesson, has these words:

"Again Jesus brings forth the promise to the victorious soul which 'overcometh.' This time the promise is broader. In Ephesus it was to eat of the tree of life, to be gifted with a blessed immortality; in Smyrna it was to be safe from the second death: in Pergamos it was to be fed with the heavenly food and to be chosen to the new name and condition of heavenly dignity; in Thyatira it was to share in Jesus' power over all nations, wearing the starry crown; here in Sardis it is the white robe of a heavenly purity of heart and life, a perpetual lease of the heavenly life, and Jesus' own glorious confession of him before the great throne of the infinite Father, and before the splendid assembly of his angels."

These consolations, addressed in such varied form to the faithful ones of the different churches, had for each a peculiar meaning. We have to study the special wants and sufferings of each, to fully understand the meaning of each blessed promise.

But those ancient churches and Christians are only the representatives of all Christians in all times. The warnings, the incentives, the promises, the consolations, are as much for us, in their fullest meaning, as they were for them. Do we study them that we may apply them to our own hearts, and lives, and hopes of the future?

Singing. "Beautiful Zion."—Happy Voices, p. 213; or,

Glorious things of thee are spoken
Zion city of our God.

CHURCH OF PHILADELPHIA.

CLASS E.

Supt. What are Christ's titles in the message to this church?

First Pupil. "And to the angel of the church in Philadelphia write: These things saith he that is holy, he that is true, he that hath the key of David, he that openeth, and no man shutteth; and shutteth, and no man openeth."

Supt. What is set before this church, and why?

Second Pupil. "I know thy works: Behold, I have set before thee an open door, and no man can shut it: for thou hast a little strength, and hast kept my word, and hast not denied my name."

Supt. What is the explanation of this?

Third Pupil. I think the open door means an opportunity for usefulness and an assured reward; and the little strength means that the talent given has been improved.

Fourth Pupil. I have an illustration. It is in the parable of the "talents."

"His Lord said unto him, Well done, good and faithful servant; thou hast been faithful over a few things, I will make thee ruler over many things: enter into the joy of thy Lord."—Matt. 25 : 21.

Fifth Pupil. There is a comforting assurance contained in the 10th verse of the lesson.

"Because thou hast kept the word of my patience, I also will keep thee from the hour of temptation, which shall come upon all the world, to try them that dwell upon the earth."

Supt. And to him that overcometh, what glorious promise?

Sixth Pupil. "Him that overcometh will I make a pillar in the temple of my God, and he shall go no more out: and I will write upon him the name of my God, and the name of the city of my God, which is new Jerusalem, which cometh down out of heaven from my God: and I will write upon him my new name."

Supt. "The name of my God."

Seventh Pupil. "And I looked, and lo, a Lamb stood on the Mount Zion, and with him an hundred forty and four thousand, having his father's name written in their foreheads."—Rev. 14 : 1.

Supt. "And the name of the city of my God."

Eighth Pupil. "And I, John, saw the holy city, new Jerusalem, coming down from God out of heaven, prepared as a bride adorned for her husband."—Rev. 21 : 2.

Supt. "The pillar in the temple of my God."

The beauty and perfection of architecture is often used by the pen of inspiration to represent the harmony and completeness of spiritual things. What a place do the tabernacle and the temple hold in the ancient revelation of God to man! And the New Testament gives us the "foundation," the "corner stone," the "house," "the whole building fitly joined together."

"The temple of my God!" Think of it, faithful Christian; what exaltation is this! This temple is the great consummation of God's work. The universe was made for this; yet the humble follower of Christ, if faithful to the end, shall stand a beautiful pillar in this glorious temple forever. This sinful world is the dark quarry whence all the stones of the building are hewn, and by and by, in the light of that brighter day, we shall see that our trials here were all needed to make the pillars and all the "living stones" fit for a place in that glorious building.

"To him that overcometh." There is, then, a contest with a victory possible, and a glorious, eternal reward. Here is Paul's testimony concerning his earthly warfare and heavenly crown. He says: "I have fought a good fight, I have finished my course, I have kept the faith; henceforth there is laid up for me a crown of righteousness, which the Lord, the righteous judge shall give me at that day; and not to me only but unto all them that love his appearing."

Singing. "My home is there."—Fresh Laurels, p. 95; or,

Jerusalem my happy home.

Recitation by four pupils from infant class.

1 Jesus, high in glory,
Lend a listening ear;
When we bow before thee,
Infant praises hear.

2 We are little children,
Weak and apt to stray;
Saviour, guide and keep us
In the heavenly way.

3 Save us, Lord, from sinning,
Watch us day by day;
Help us now to love thee,
Take our sins away.

4 Then, when Jesus calls us
To our heavenly home,
We will answer gladly,
Saviour, Lord, we come.

THE CHURCH OF LAODICEA.

CLASS F.

Supt. What does Jesus say of this church, and what does he mean by it?

First Pupil. "I know thy works, that thou art neither cold nor hot: I would thou wert cold or hot. So then because thou art lukewarm, and neither cold nor hot, I will spew thee out of my mouth."

It means that Jesus hates indifference, and loves earnestness in his cause.

Second Pupil. I have an illustrative text.

"And when he saw a fig-tree in the way, he came to it, and found nothing thereon, but leaves only, and said unto it, Let no fruit grow on thee henceforward forever; and presently the fig-tree withered away."—Matt. 21: 19.

Teacher. Nothing but leaves; the Spirit grieves
Over a wasted life,
O'er sin committed while conscience slept,
Promises made but never kept,
Folly and shame and strife;
Nothing but leaves.

Supt. Why was this church indifferent?

Third Pupil. Because its members were rich and proud, and thought themselves righteous when they were not.

"Because thou sayest, I am rich, and increased with goods, and have need of nothing; and knowest not that thou art wretched, and miserable, and poor, and blind, and naked."

Supt. What does Jesus counsel them to do?

Fourth Pupil. To come to him for true spiritual riches.

"I counsel thee to buy of me gold tried in the fire, that thou mayest be rich; and white raiment that thou mayest be clothed, and that the shame of thy nakedness do not appear; and anoint thine eyes with eye-salve, that thou mayest see."

Supt. What is the Saviour's attitude towards the sinner?

Fifth Pupil. "Behold, I stand at the door, and knock; if any man hear my voice, and open the door, I will come in to him, and will sup with him, and he with me."

A Teacher. Behold a stranger at the door:
He gently knocks, has knocked before;
Has waited long, is waiting still;
You treat no other friend so ill.

Supt. What final promise does the Saviour make to those who overcome?

Sixth Pupil. "To him that overcometh will I grant to sit with me in my throne, even as I also overcame, and am set down with my Father in his throne."

RECITATION.

1 Soon and forever — such promise our trust,
Though ashes to ashes, and dust go to dust;
Soon and forever — our union shall be
Made perfect and glorious, Redeemer, with thee.

2 When the sins and the sorrows of time shall be o'er,
Its pangs and its partings remembered no more;
Where life cannot fail, and where death cannot sever;
Christians with Christ shall be soon and forever.

3 Soon and forever — the work shall be done,
The warfare accomplished, the victory won;
Soon and forever — the soldier lay down
His sword for a harp, and his cross for a crown.

4 Then droop not in sorrow, despair not in fear,
A glorious to-morrow is brightening, is near;
When, blessed reward of each faithful endeavor!
Christians with Christ shall be soon and forever.

Singing.

SONG OF THE CELESTIAL COUNTRY.

1 Jerusalem the golden,
With milk and honey blest,
Beneath thy contemplation,
Sink heart and voice to rest.

I know not—oh! I know not
What joys await me there,
What radiancy of glory,
What bliss beyond compare.

2 They stand, those halls of Zion,
All jubilant with song,
And bright with many an angel,
And all the martyr throng.
There is the throne of David,
And there, from toil released,
The shout of them that triumph,
The song of them that feast.

3 And they who, with their Leader,
Have conquered in the fight,
For ever and for ever
Are clad in robes of white.
Oh, land that seest no sorrow,
Oh, state that fear'st no strife,
Oh, royal land of flowers,
Oh, realms and home of life!

4 Oh, sweet and blessed country,
The home of God's elect,
Oh, sweet and blessed country,
That eager hearts expect!
Jesus, in mercy bring us
To that dear land of rest,
Who art, with God the Father
And Spirit, ever blest.

Pastor. Prayer and Benediction.

XV.

The Cross and the Crown:

A LESSON OF SALVATION.

"In the world ye shall have tribulation; but be of good cheer; I have overcome the world."—*John* 16: 33.

"Be thou faithful unto death, and I will give thee a crown of life."
— *Rev.* 2: 10.

EXERCISE.

Opening Hymn. Notes of Joy, p. 62 (or substitute).

We gather in this dear retreat
To worship at the Saviour's feet.

Supt. and School. The Lord's Prayer.

Song. "Children's Saviour." — Fresh Laurels, p. 4 (or substitute).

SCRIPTURE READING.

Supt. read, concerning Christ's Humiliation, Luke 22 : 39–44.

Pastor read, concerning Christ's Exaltation, Heb. 1 : 1–8.

PRAYER BY PASTOR.

Song. "The Lamb that was slain."—Fresh Laurels, No. 27 (or substitute).

(*Here one or two extra songs, with solo and chorus, or quartette and chorus, for variety, or a recitation or dialogue by a little class from the infant department, may be introduced or omitted, according to amount of time.*)

THE CROSS AND THE CROWN, IN FOUR PARTS

PART I.—CHRIST'S HUMILIATION.

Supt. What are the words of Scripture concerning the cross of Christ?

A Teacher. "And as Moses lifted up the serpent in the wilderness, even so must the Son of Man be lifted up."—John 3 : 14.

First Pupil. "And I, if I be lifted up from the earth, will draw all men unto me."—John 12 : 32.

Second Pupil. "This he said, signifying what death he should die."—John 12 : 33.

Third Pupil. "And Judas Iscariot, one of the twelve, went unto the chief priests, to betray him unto them."—Mark 14 : 10.

Fourth Pupil. "Yea, mine own familiar friend, in whom I trusted, which did eat of my bread, hath lifted up his heel against me."—Ps. 41 : 19.

Fifth Pupil. "Then cometh Jesus with them unto a place called Gethsemane, and saith unto his disciples, Sit ye here, while I go and pray, yonder."—Matt. 26 : 36.

Sixth Pupil. "Then saith he unto them, My soul is exceeding sorrowful, even unto death ; tarry ye here, and watch with me."—Matt. 26 : 38.

Seventh Pupil. "And he went a little further, and fell on his face, and prayed, saying, O my Father, if it be possible, let this cup pass from me ! Nevertheless, not as I will, but as thou wilt."—Matt. 26 : 39.

Eighth Pupil. "And there appeared an angel unto him from heaven, strengthening him."—Luke 22 : 43.

Ninth Pupil. "And being in an agony he prayed more earnestly, and his sweat was as it were great drops of blood falling down to the ground."—Luke 22 : 44.

Supt. or a Teacher. "Surely, he hath borne our griefs and carried our sorrows ; yet we did esteem him stricken, smitten of God, and afflicted."—Is. 53 : 4.

Ass't Supt. or a Teacher. "But he was wounded for our transgressions, he was bruised for our iniquities, the chastisement of our peace was upon him, and with his stripes we are healed."—Is. 53 : 5.

A Lady Teacher.

Go to dark Gethsemane,
  Ye that feel the tempter's power;
Your Redeemer's conflict see,
  Watch with him one bitter hour;
Turn not from his griefs away,—
  Learn of Jesus Christ to pray.

Tenth Pupil. "Then the band, and the captain, and the officers of the Jews, took Jesus, and bound him."—John 18 : 12.

Eleventh Pupil. "Now the chief priests and elders, and all the council, sought false witnesses against Jesus, to put him to death."—Matt. 26 : 59.

Twelfth Pupil. "And when he was accused of the chief priests and elders, he answered nothing."—Matt. 27 : 12.

Supt. "He was oppressed and he was afflicted, yet he opened not his mouth; he is brought as a lamb to the slaughter, and as a sheep before her shearers is dumb, so he openeth not his mouth."—Is. 53 : 7.

A Teacher. "He was taken from prison and from judgment, and who shall declare his generation? For he was cut off out of the land of the living; for the transgression of my people was he stricken."—Is. 53 : 8.

Another. "Pilate saith unto them, What shall I do, then, with Jesus, which is called the Christ? They all say unto him, Let him be crucified."—Matt. 27 : 22.

Thirteenth Pupil. "Then released he Barabbas unto them; and when he had scourged Jesus, he delivered him to be crucified."—Matt. 27 : 26.

Fourteenth Pupil. "And when they had platted a crown of thorns, they put it upon his head, and a reed in his right hand; and they bowed the knee before him, and mocked him, saying, Hail, King of the Jews!"—Matt. 27 : 29.

A Teacher. "He is despised and rejected of men, a man of sorrows, and acquainted with grief, and we hid as it were our faces from him; he was despised, and we esteemed him not."—Is. 53 : 3.

Fifteenth Pupil. "And after that they had mocked him, they took the robe off from him, and put his own raiment on him, and led him away, to crucify him."—Matt. 27: 31.

Sixteenth Pupil. "And he, bearing his cross, went forth into a place called the place of the skull, which is called in the Hebrew Golgotha."—John xix. 17.

Seventeenth Pupil. "And when they were come to the place which is called Calvary, there they crucified him and the malefactors, one on the right hand, and the other on the left."—Luke 23: 33.

A Lady. When I survey the wondrous cross,
On which the Prince of Glory died,
My richest gain I count but loss,
And pour contempt on all my pride.

Were the whole realm of nature mine,
That were a present far too small;
Love so amazing, so divine,
Demands my soul, my life, my all.

A Teacher. "Then said Jesus, Father, forgive them, for they know not what they do. And they parted his raiment, and cast lots."—Luke 23: 34.

Eighteenth Pupil. "And it was about the sixth hour; and there was a darkness over all the earth until the ninth hour."—Luke 23: 44.

Nineteenth Pupil. "And behold, the vail of the temple was rent in twain, from the top to the bottom, and the earth did quake, and the rocks rent."—Matt. 27: 51.

Twentieth Pupil. "And about the ninth hour Jesus cried with a loud voice, saying, Eli, Eli, lama sabacthani? that is to say, My God, my God, why hast thou forsaken me?"—Matt. 27: 46.

Twenty-first Pupil. "And when Jesus had cried with a loud voice, he said, Father, into thy hands I commend my spirit."—Luke 23: 46.

Congregation sing four verses,

There is a fountain filled with blood.

PART II.—CHRIST'S EXALTATION.

Supt. What concerning the Saviour's crown?

Teacher.

Jesus, our Head, once crowned with thorns,
  Is crowned with glory now;
Heaven's royal diadem adorns
  The mighty victor's brow.

Twenty-second Pupil. "In the end of the Sabbath, as it began to dawn toward the first day of the week, came Mary Magdalene and the other Mary to see the sepulchre."—Matt. 28: 1.

Twenty-third Pupil. "And the angel answered and said to the women, Fear not ye, for I know that ye seek Jesus, which was crucified."—Matt. 28: 5.

Twenty-fourth Pupil. "Whom God hath raised up, having loosed the pains of death, because it was not possible that he should be holden of it."—Acts 2: 24.

Twenty-fifth Pupil. "He is not here, for he is risen, as he said. Come see the place where the Lord lay."—Matt. 28: 6.

Twenty-sixth Pupil. "Therefore, let all the house of Israel know assuredly that God hath made that same Jesus, whom ye have crucified, both Lord and Christ."—Acts 2: 36.

Twenty-seventh Pupil. "And I looked, and behold, a white cloud, and upon the cloud one sat like unto the Son of Man, having on his head a golden crown, and in his hand a sharp sickle."—Rev. 14: 14.

Twenty-eighth Pupil. "And I saw, and behold, a white horse, and he that sat on him had a bow, and a crown was given unto him; and he went forth, conquering and to conquer."—Rev. 6: 2.

Twenty-ninth Pupil. "But we see Jesus, who was made a little lower than the angels for the suffering of death, crowned with glory and honor, that he, by the grace of God, should taste death for every man."—Heb. 2: 9.

Thirtieth Pupil. "But unto the Son he saith, Thy throne, O God, is forever and ever; a scepter of righteousness is the scepter of thy kingdom."—Heb. 1: 8.

Supt. or Asst. Supt. "For unto us a child is born, unto us a son is given, and the government shall be upon his shoulder; and his name shall be called Wonderful, Counselor, The Mighty God, The Everlasting Father, The Prince of Peace."—Is. 9 . 6.

Congregation sing "Coronation:"

All hail the power of Jesus' name!

PART III.—THE CHRISTIAN'S CROSS.

Supt. What concerning the Christian's cross?

A Lady Teacher.

Dear Lamb of God, enhance thy cross
More and yet more; all else is dross.
Let ne'er a murmur mar my rest,—
Plant thy own patience in my breast,
To guard me, faith, hope, love combine,
Until the glorious crown be mine.
— *Cross Bearer.*

Thirty-first Pupil. "And he said to them all, If any man will come after me let him deny himself, and take up his cross daily, and follow me."—Luke 9: 23.

Thirty-second Pupil. "And he that taketh not his cross, and followeth after me, is not worthy of me."—Matt. 10: 38.

Thirty-third Pupil. "Then Jesus beholding him, loved him, and said unto him, One thing thou lackest; go thy way, sell whatsoever thou hast, and give to the poor, and thou shalt have treasure in heaven; and come, take up thy cross and follow me."—Mark 10: 21.

Thirty-fourth Pupil. "But God forbid that I should glory, save in the cross of our Lord Jesus Christ, by whom the world is crucified unto me, and I unto the world."—Gal. 6: 14.

Thirty-fifth Pupil "Wherefore, seeing we also are compassed about with so great a cloud of witnesses, let us lay aside every weight, and the sin which doth so easily beset us, and let us run with patience the race that is set before us."—Heb. 12 1

Thirty-sixth Pupil. "Looking unto Jesus, the author and finisher of our faith, who, for the joy that was set before him, endured the cross, despising the shame, and is set down at the right hand of the throne of God"—Heb. 12. 2.

Member Ladies' Bible Class. We may be weary under the cross, but should never be weary *of* it. Labors for our blessed Master are but a poor return for all his love, his labors and sacrifices for us. And yet they are the best we can tender. They are the return he looks for, after all his care in planting us as fig-trees in his vineyard, and in providing for and cultivating us.

"Bear much fruit; so shall ye be my disciples."

Another Member. "Weary of the cross? Oh, cowardice! Oh, effeminacy! unworthy of him who aspires to the glory and joy of heaven! Demas was weary of it, because it embarrassed the eager pursuit of the world, to which he had abandoned himself."

Another. "We should never cease from our conflicts while we remain where there is still one of Christ's enemies to be subdued, or one soul to be saved by our faithful labors."

Another. "We should never forget the animating words of the apostle, speaking in his Master's name: 'Let us not be weary in well-doing, for in due season we shall reap, if we faint not.'"— *Cross Bearer.*

Congregation sing "Olivet,"

My faith looks up to Thee.

PART IV.— THE CHRISTIAN'S CROWN.

Supt. What concerning the Christian's crown?

Teacher. 'In that day shall the Lord of Hosts be for a crown of glory and for a diadem of beauty unto the residue of the people."— Is. 28: 5.

Thirty-seventh Pupil. "For what is our hope, or joy, or crown of rejoicing? Are not even ye in the presence of our Lord Jesus Christ at his coming?"— 1 Thess. 2. 19.

Thirty-eighth Pupil. "Behold, I come quickly, hold that fast which thou hast, that no man take thy crown."— Rev. 3. 11.

Thirty-ninth Pupil. "And when the Chief Shepherd shall appear, ye shall receive a crown of glory, that fadeth not away." — 1 Peter 5: 4.

Fortieth Pupil. "Blessed is the man that endureth temptation, for when he is tried, he shall receive the crown of life, which the Lord hath promised to them that love him."—James 1: 12.

Forty-first Pupil. "Fear none of those things which thou shalt suffer. Behold, the devil shall cast some of you into prison, that ye may be tried, and ye shall have tribulation ten days: Be thou faithful unto death, and I will give thee a crown of life."—Rev. 2: 10.

Forty-second Pupil. "Now, if we be dead with Christ, we believe that we shall also live with him."—Rom. 6: 8.

Forty-third Pupil. "Every man that striveth for the mastery is temperate in all things. Now, they do it to obtain a corruptible crown, but we an incorruptible."—1 Cor. 9: 25.

Forty-fourth Pupil. "To him that overcometh, will I grant to sit with me in my throne, even as I also overcame, and am set down with my Father in his throne."—Rev. 3: 21.

Forty-fifth Pupil. "I have fought a good fight; I have finished my course; I have kept the faith."—2 Tim. 4: 7.

Forty-sixth Pupil. "Henceforth there is laid up for me a crown of righteousness, which the Lord, the Righteous Judge, shall give me at that day; and not to me only, but unto all them, also, that love his appearing."—2 Tim. 4: 8.

Singing. "Beautiful Mansions."—Fresh Laurels, p. 9 (or substitute.)

BRIEF REMARKS BY THE PASTOR.

THE WAY TO THE HILL.*

A child walking with his father one fine sunny morning, asked that they might go to the top of a distant hill, in order that he might look at the beautiful prospect which was to be seen from thence. His father promised to comply with his request, and they went on. But the way which led to the hill was long and tedious; the sun's rays were very powerful,

* Cross and Crown series.

and there were no trees to afford a welcome shade; the ground was hard and stony, and hurt their feet; and when they came to a winding part of the road, they lost sight of the hill altogether.

The boy's patience was quite exhausted; his courage failed him; and, sitting down upon the ground, he began to cry, and to complain that his father, instead of gratifying his wish, had led him along such a hot, dusty wearisome path—a path which appeared interminable. "It is very unkind of you, father," he murmured, "to disappoint me in this way. I asked you to let me look at the beautiful scenery to be seen from the top of that hill, and you have only brought me here, where all is dull, and dreary, and vexatious."

"My child," answered the father gently, "this is the way to the hill; you cannot get there without going by this road."

God loves his own and leads them by a road
Unerring to their goal; but he knows best
The path which leads to heaven.

Congregation sing three verses,

Must Jesus bear the cross alone?

XVI.

Angels:

A LESSON CONCERNING HEAVENLY THINGS.

"And of the angels he saith, who maketh his angels spirits, his ministers a flame of fire."—*Heb.* 1: 7.

"Likewise, I say unto you, There is joy in the presence of the angels of God over one sinner that repenteth."—Luke 15: 10.

EXERCISE.

The School and Congregation sing the Doxology.

Praise God, from whom all blessings flow,
Praise him, all creatures here below,
Praise him above, ye heavenly host,
Praise Father, Son, and Holy Ghost.

PRAYER.

Closing with the Lord's Prayer, in which the whole school joins.

Supt.
Praise ye the Lord, praise ye the Lord from the heavens;
Praise him in the heights.

School. Praise ye him, all his angels;
Praise ye him, all his hosts.

Choir and School chant the "Gloria Patri."
(*See Appendix.*)

RESPONSIVE READING.

The 91st Psalm.

Supt. "He that dwelleth in the secret place of the Most High shall abide under the shadow of the Almighty."

School. "I will say of the Lord, He is my refuge and my fortress: my God; in him will I trust."
(*To the end of the Psalm.*)

Singing. "Beautiful Land of Song."— Pure Gold, p. 64.

"And they sung as it were a new song."—Rev. 14: 3.

1 There's a beautiful land of song,
Away o'er Jordan's river,
Where saints, a happy white-robed throng,
Their notes in joyful strains prolong,
In praise to God forever.

CHORUS.— In that beautiful land of song,
Ransomed ones are singing;
O'er hill and plain with sweet refrain,
The glad new song is ringing.

2 We have heard of the blest ones there,
Who live beside the river,
They bloom in beauty, young and fair,
And crowns of life immortal wear,
And sing and shout forever.

CHORUS.

3 Jesus reigns in that goodly land,
He leaves his people never,
Around his throne a radiant band
With palms of victory in their hand,
His children sing forever.

CHORUS.

4 We shall meet on that blissful shore,
Where time no more will sever,
When earthly toils and cares are o'er.
We'll join with loved ones gone before,
And sing of Christ forever.

CHORUS.

Superintendent announce the subject and begin the lesson with

CLASS A.

Supt. What is contained in the Scriptures concerning the rank or position of angels among created beings?

First Pupil. "For thou hast made him a little lower than the angels, and hast crowned him with glory and honor."— Ps. 8: 5.

Supt. What is the meaning of Angel? And what names of angels have we in the Bible?

Second Pupil. Angel means a messenger, and we have given in the Bible, the names, Gabriel, which means the strength of God; and Michael, which means the prince of the armies of God.

Supt. What concerning the home of the angels?

Third Pupil. "And he said, Hear thou therefore the word of the Lord · I saw the Lord sitting on his throne, and all the host of heaven standing by him on his right hand and on his left."—1 Kings 22. 19.

Supt. What concerning the employment of the angels?

Fourth Pupil. "But to which of the angels said he at any time Sit on my right hand, until I make thine enemies thy footstool? Are they not all ministering spirits, sent forth to minister for them who shall be heirs of salvation?"—Heb. 1: 13, 14.

Supt. There is in the Book of Job something about the existence of angels at the time of the earth's creation.

Fifth Pupil. "Where wast thou when I laid the foundations of the earth, declare, if thou hast understanding: When the morning stars sang together, and all the sons of God shouted for joy?"—Job 38: 4, 7.

Supt. When Adam and Eve were banished from the garden of Eden, what service did angels perform?

Sixth Pupil. "So he drove out the man: and he placed at the east of the garden of Eden cherubim, and a flaming sword which turned every way to keep the way of the tree of life."—Gen. 3. 24.

(*Read from the 103d Psalm, responsive.*)

Supt. "But the mercy of the Lord is from everlasting to everlasting upon them that fear him, and his righteousness unto children's children."

Teachers. "To such as keep his covenant, and to those that remember his commandments to do them."

Supt. "The Lord hath prepared his throne in the heavens; and his kingdom ruleth over all."

Teachers. "Bless the Lord, ye his angels, that excel in strength, that do his commandments, hearkening unto the voice of his word."

Supt. "Bless ye the Lord, all ye his hosts, ye ministers of his, that do his pleasure."

Teachers. "Bless the Lord, all his works in all places of his dominion: bless the Lord, O my soul."

Chant. "Praise the Lord." (*See Appendix.*)

Supt. CLASS B will tell us some Bible instances of the ministrations of angels.

First Pupil. The prophet Daniel was saved from a cruel death at the hands of his enemies.

"Then said Daniel unto the king, O king, live for ever: My God hath sent his angel, and hath shut the lions' mouths, that they have not hurt me: forasmuch as before him innocency was found in me; and also before thee, O king, have I done no hurt."— Daniel 6: 21, 22.

Second Pupil. Elijah was carefully ministered unto by angels when a fugitive from the wrath of Queen Jezebel.

"But he himself went a day's journey into the wilderness, and came and sat down under a juniper tree: and he requested for himself that he might die; and said, It is enough; now, O Lord, take away my life; for I am not better than my fathers." — 1 Kings 19: 4.

Third Pupil. "And as he lay and slept under a juniper tree, behold, then an angel touched him, and said unto him, Arise and eat."—1 Kings 19: 5.

Fourth Pupil. "And he looked, and behold there was a cake baken on the coals, and a cruse of water at his head. And he did eat and drink, and laid him down again."— 1 Kings 19: 6.

Fifth Pupil. "And the angel of the Lord came again the second time, and touched him, and said, Arise and eat; because the journey is too great for thee."— 1 Kings 19: 7.

Sixth Pupil. "And he arose, and did eat and drink, and went in the strength of that meat forty days and forty nights unto Horeb the mount of God."— 1 Kings 19: 8.

Seventh Pupil. There was a beautiful exhibition of angels to Jacob, in the dream which he had at Bethel.

"And he dreamed, and behold a ladder set up on the earth, and the top of it reached to heaven: and behold the angels of God ascending and descending on it."— Gen. 28: 12.

RECITATION.

1 Ah! many a time we look on star-lit nights
Up to the sky, as Jacob did of old,
Look longing up to the eternal lights
To spell their lives of gold.

2 But never more, as to the Hebrew boy,
Each on his way, the angels walk abroad,
And never more we hear with aweful joy,
The audible voice of God.

3 Yet to the pure eyes the ladder is still set,
And angel visitants still come and go;
Many bright messengers are moving yet
From the dark world below.

4 Spirits elect, through suffering rendered meet
For those high mansions — from the nursery-door,
Bright babes that seem to climb with clay-cold feet,
Up to the golden floor.

5 These are the messengers, forever wending
From earth to Heaven, that faith alone may scan,
These are the angels of God, ascending
Upon the Son of Man.

Singing. "Songs of the Unseen."— The Charm, p. 140.

1 If we only sought to brighten,
Every pathway dark with care,
If we only tried to lighten,
All the burdens others bear,
CHORUS.— We should hear the angels, hear the angels singing,
All around us night and day:
Yes, we should feel the gentle angels winging
At our side their upward way.

2 If we only strove to cherish
   Every pure and holy thought;
 Till within our hearts should perish
   All that is with evil fraught,
CHORUS.

3 If we only did our duty.
   Thinking not what it might cost,
 Then the earth would wear new beauty,
   Fair as that in Eden lost.
CHORUS.

Supt. CLASS C will give us some account of the ministrations of angels in connection with the Saviour's birth.

First Pupil. It is recorded in the 1st and 2d chapters of Luke.

"And in the sixth month the angel Gabriel was sent from God unto a city of Galilee named Nazareth: To a virgin espoused to a man whose name was Joseph, of the house of David: and the virgin's name was Mary."—Luke 1: 26, 27.

Second Pupil. "And the angel came in unto her, and said, Hail, thou that art highly favored, the Lord is with thee: blessed art thou among women."—Luke 1: 28.

Third Pupil. "And when she saw him, she was troubled at his saying, and cast in her mind what manner of salutation this should be."—Luke 1. 29.

Fourth Pupil. "And the angel said unto her, Fear not, Mary: for thou hast found favor with God: And, behold, thou shalt conceive in thy womb and bring forth a son, and shalt call his name JESUS."—Luke 1: 30, 31.

Fifth Pupil. "And there were in the same country shepherds abiding in the field, keeping watch over their flock by night."—Luke 2: 8.

Sixth Pupil. "And, lo, the angel of the Lord came upon them, and the glory of the Lord shone round about them; and they were sore afraid."—Luke 2: 9.

Seventh Pupil. "And the angel said unto them, Fear not: for, behold, I bring you good tidings of great joy, which shall be to all people: For unto you is born this day in the city of David a Saviour which is Christ the Lord: And suddenly there was with the angel a multitude of the heavenly host praising God, and saying: Glory to God in the highest, and on earth peace, good will toward men."—Luke 2: 10, 11, 13, 14.

Supt. Were there other instances of the ministrations of angels upon Christ?

Teacher. There were. After the forty days' temptation in the wilderness, "angels came and ministered unto him."

After the agony in the garden of Gethsemane, "there appeared an angel unto him from heaven, strengthening him."

Angels also rolled away the stone from the sepulchre.

Singing. "The Christmas Hymn."—Happy Voices, p. 158.

Christ is born, and heaven rejoices,
  Judah's plains are bathed in light,
Thousand, thousand harps and voices,
  Break the silence of the night.
CHORUS.—Glory in the highest, glory,
  Peace on earth, good will to men.

Supt. CLASS D will tell us of the angels as guardians of nations and individuals.

First Pupil. "But the prince of the kingdom of Persia withstood me one and twenty days: but, lo, Michael, one of the chief princes, came to help me; and I remained there with the kings of Persia."—Dan. 10: 13.

Second Pupil. "The angel of the Lord encampeth round about them that fear him, and delivereth them."—Ps. 34: 7.

Third Pupil. "And Elisha prayed, and said, Lord, I pray thee, open his eyes, that he may see. And the Lord opened the eyes of the young man; and he saw; and, behold, the mountain was full of horses and chariots of fire round about Elisha."—2 Kings 6: 17.

Fourth Pupil. "Behold, I send an angel before thee, to keep thee in the way, and to bring thee into the place which I have prepared."—Ex. 23: 20.

Fifth Pupil. "For he shall give his angels charge over thee, to keep thee in all thy ways: They shall bear thee up in their hands, lest thou dash thy foot against a stone."—Ps. 91: 11, 12.

Teacher. Jesus, my Lord, my living friend,
May these thy servants me attend,
Through life: and when I quit this clay,
Safe to thine arms my soul convey.

Supt. CLASS E will tell us something about the angels, as to their number, and their services to God and to us.

First Pupil. Daniel says of the "Ancient of Days," "Thousand thousands ministered unto him, and ten thousand times ten thousand stood before him."— Dan. 7: 10.

Second Pupil. Christ said:
"Thinkest thou that I cannot now pray to my Father, and he shall presently give me more than twelve legions of angels?" — Matt. 26: 53.

Third Pupil. The Psalmist declares:
"The chariots of God are twenty thousand, even thousands of angels: the Lord is among them, as in Sinai, in the holy place."— Ps. 68: 17.

Fourth Pupil. Paul says:
"But ye are come unto Mount Zion, and unto the city of the living God, the heavenly Jerusalem, and to an innumerable company of angels."— Heb. 12: 22.

Fifth Pupil. "To the general assembly and church of the firstborn, which are written in heaven, and to God the Judge of all, and to the spirits of just men made perfect."

Sixth Pupil. "And to Jesus the mediator of the new covenant, and to the blood of sprinkling, that speaketh better things than that of Abel."

Seventh Pupil. "See that ye refuse not him that speaketh; for if they escaped not who refused him that spake on earth, much more shall not we escape, if we turn away from him that speaketh from heaven."

Supt. What is the great source of joy to this innumerable company of angels?

Teacher. "Likewise, I say unto you, there is joy in the presence of the angels of God over one sinner that repenteth." —Luke 15: 10.

Singing. "Let the good angels come in."—Fresh Laurels, p. 122.

They hover around us, bright angels are near,
  To glory immortal they win,
Then gladly we'll open the door of our hearts,
  And let the good angels come in.

RECITATION.

THE UNDISCOVERED COUNTRY.

1 Could we but know
The land that ends our dark, uncertain travel,
  Where lie those happier hills and meadows low;
Ah! if beyond the spirit's inmost cavil
  Aught of that country could we really know,
    Who would not go?

2 Might we but hear
The hovering angels' high imagined chorus,
  Or catch, betimes, with wakeful eyes and clear,
One radiant vista of the realm before us,
  With one rapt moment given to see and hear,
    Ah! who would fear?

3 Were we quite sure
To find the peerless friend, who left us lonely,
  Or there, by some celestial stream as pure,
To gaze in eyes that here were love-lit only—
  This weary mortal evil, were we quite sure,
    Who would endure? —*Round Table.*

RECITATION.

And now the air
Grew tremulous with heavenly melody,
Far-off at first it seems, and indistinct,
As swells and sinks the multitudinous roar
Of ocean; but ere long the waves of sound
Rolled on articulate, and then I knew
The voice of harpers harping on their harps.
And lo, upon the extreme verge of cloud,
As one at Eden's portals, there appeared
A company of angels clothed in light;
Thronging the path, or in the amber air
Suspense. And in the twinkling of an eye

We were among them, and they clustered round,
And waved their wings, and struck their harps again,
For gladness; every look was tenderness,
And every word was musical with joy.
Welcome to heaven, dear brother, welcome home!
Welcome to thine inheritance of light!
Welcome forever to thy Master's joy!
Thy work is done, thy pilgrimage is past;
Thy guardian angel's vigil is fulfilled;
Thy parents wait thee in the bowers of bliss;
Thy infant babes have woven wreaths for thee;
Thy brethren who have entered into rest
Long for thy coming; and the angel choirs
Are ready with their symphonies of praise.
Nor shall thy voice be mute; a golden harp
For thee is hanging on the trees of life;
And sweetly shall its chords forever ring,
Responsive to thy touch of ecstacy,
With hallelujahs to thy Lord and ours.

From "Yesterday, To-day, and Forever."

Singing. "The Shining Way."— Happy Voices, p. 187.

The pearly gates are open wide.

XVII.

Our Heavenly Home:

A LESSON OF VICTORY.

"These are they which came out of great tribulation, and have washed their robes, and made them white in the blood of the Lamb."

"Blessed are they that do his commandments, that they may have right to the tree of life and may enter in through the gates into the city."—*Rev.* 22: 14.

EXERCISE.

Opening Song. "March, March to Glory." — Notes of Joy, p. 55 (or substitute).

SCRIPTURE READING.

Supt. "Who shall separate us from the love of Christ? shall tribulation, or distress, or persecution, or famine, or nakedness, or peril, or sword? As it is written, For thy sake we are killed all the day long; we are accounted as sheep for the slaughter." — Romans 8: 35, 36.

Asst. Supt. "Nay, in all these things we are more than conquerors through him that loved us. For I am persuaded, that neither death, nor life, nor angels, nor principalities, nor powers, nor things present, nor things to come. nor height, nor depth, nor any other creature, shall be able to separate us from the love of God, which is in Christ Jesus our Lord."— Romans 8: 37–39.

Supt. "He that hath an ear, let him hear what the Spirit saith unto the churches; To him that overcometh will I give to eat of the tree of life, which is in the midst of the paradise of God. He that hath an ear, let him hear what the Spirit saith unto the churches; He that overcometh shall not be hurt of the second death. He that hath an ear, let him hear what the Spirit saith unto the churches; To him that overcometh will I give to eat of the hidden manna, and will give him a white stone, and in the stone a new name written, which no man knoweth saving he that receiveth it. And he that overcometh, and keepeth my works unto the end, to him will I give power over the nations."— Rev. 2: 7, 11, 17, 26.

Asst. Supt. "He that overcometh, the same shall be clothed in white raiment; and I will not blot out his name out of the book of life, but I will confess his name before my Father, and before his angels. Him that overcometh will I make a pillar in the temple of my God, and he shall go no more out: and I will write upon him the name of my God, and the name of the city of my God, which is New Jerusalem, which cometh down out of heaven from my God: and I will write upon him my new name. To him that overcometh will I grant to sit with me in my throne, even as I also overcame, and am set down with my Father in his throne. He that hath an ear, let him hear what the Spirit saith unto the churches."—Rev. 3: 5, 12, 21, 22.

Supt. "So when this corruptible shall have put on incorruption, and this mortal shall have put on immortality, then shall be brought to pass the saying that is written, Death is swallowed up in victory. O death, where is thy sting? O grave, where is thy victory? The sting of death is sin; and the strength of sin is the law. But thanks be to God, which giveth us the victory through our Lord Jesus Christ."—1 Cor. 15: 54–57.

Choir and School sing "Happy Home."

(*See Appendix.*)

PRAYER BY THE PASTOR.

(*With special reference to the subject of the exercise.*)

Song. "Our Victory."—Fresh Laurels, p. 120.
Or, "Strike, Strike for Victory."—Pure Gold, p. 96.

BRIEF ADDRESS

By the Pastor to the children, familiar and illustrative, using the following text:

"Wherefore, seeing we also are compassed about with so great a cloud of witnesses, let us lay aside every weight, and the sin which doth so easily beset us; and let us run with patience the race that is set before us, looking unto Jesus the author and finisher of our faith."—Heb. 12: 1

Class A.

Supt. What is the great and final blessing and reward which God promises to those who love him and are faithful in his service unto death?

Teacher. The reward of victory; the conqueror's crown; a home in heaven. "And he said unto them, Verily I say unto you, There is no man that hath left house, or parents, or brethren, or wife, or children, for the kingdom of God's sake, who shall not receive manifold more in this present time, and in the world to come life everlasting."—Luke 18: 29, 30.

First Pupil. "For I am now ready to be offered, and the time of my departure is at hand. I have fought a good fight, I have finished my course, I have kept the faith: Henceforth there is laid up for me a crown of righteousness, which the Lord, the righteous judge, shall give me at that day: and not to me only but unto all them also that love his appearing."—2 Tim. 4: 6-8

Second Pupil. "Fear none of those things which thou shalt suffer: behold, the devil shall cast some of you into prison, that ye may be tried; and ye shall have tribulation ten days: be thou faithful unto death, and I will give thee a crown of life."—Rev. 2: 10.

Third Pupil. "He that overcometh shall inherit all things; and I will be his God, and he shall be my son."—Rev. 21: 7.

Fourth Pupil. "For we know that, if our earthly house of this tabernacle were dissolved, we have a building of God, a house not made with hands, eternal in the heavens."—2 Cor. 5: 1.

Supt. "In my Father's house are many mansions."

RECITATION

By class from Infant Department (from platform).

MANSIONS OF LIGHT.

First Pupil.

Oh, say, have you heard of the mansions of light,
  Our Saviour has gone to prepare?
Where falls not a cloud or a shadow of night;
  They tell us no sorrow is there.

Second Pupil.

Oh yes, we have heard of the mansions so bright,
And free from all sorrow and care;
Our Saviour, the Lamb, is the glory and light,
The children of Zion are there.

Third Pupil.

Oh, where is that city whose portals of gold
Are open by night and by day?
The city whose splendor can never be told,
Whose pleasures will never decay?

Fourth Pupil.

'Tis yonder, where joyful our spirits may fly,
Beyond where the bright planets roll,
Above the clear arch of the blue ether sky,
The beautiful home of the soul.

Class together.

'Tis a home where the weary may rest,
The beautiful home of the blest;
Oh come, we are bound for the mansions of light,
The beautiful home of the blest.

Singing. "The Eternal Home."—Notes of Joy, p. 86. Or, "Beautiful Land of Song."—Pure Gold, p. 64.

Class B.

Supt. Who shall wear these *crowns of glory*, and inhabit these *mansions of light?*

Teacher. "Blessed are they that do his commandments, that they may have right to the tree of life, and may enter in through the gates into the city."—Rev. 22: 14.

First Pupil. "Confirming the souls of the disciples, and exhorting them to continue in the faith, and that we must through much tribulation enter into the kingdom of God."—Acts 14. 22.

Second Pupil. "Blessed is the man that endureth temptation: for when he is tried, he shall receive the crown of life, which the Lord hath promised to them that love him."—James 1: 12.

Third Pupil. "Ye are they which have continued with me in my temptations. And I appoint unto you a kingdom, as my Father hath appointed unto me; that ye may eat and drink at my table in my kingdom, and sit on thrones judging the twelve tribes of Israel."—Luke 22: 28–30.

Fourth Pupil. "And every one that hath forsaken houses, or brethren, or sisters, or father, or mother, or wife, or children, or lands, for my name's sake, shall receive a hundredfold, and shall inherit everlasting life. But many that are first shall be last; and the last shall be first."—Matt. 19: 29, 30.

Supt. What is the name of this final home of ours, and these beautiful mansions?

Fifth Pupil. "And I John saw the holy city, new Jerusalem, coming down from God out of heaven, prepared as a bride adorned for her husband."—Rev. 21: 2.

Supt. The figure of a great and beautiful city has been given us by inspiration as a faint illustration of the beauty and grandeur and gloriousness of the heavenly home of the children of God. But we know that in all things it is beyond human conception or anticipation. No human eye has seen it; no human mind can comprehend or describe it. It is the city of God. He is the architect and builder. It is the consummation of his wisdom and his love. It shall be to us a happy eternal home. Within its gates shall come no pain nor sorrow, and naught but peace and happiness shall ever enter there. The apostle John was permitted a vision of it, and, in the Book of Revelation he has given us some illustrations of its beauty and perfection. It is an "object lesson" of heavenly things given in human language to the infant class in God's great school of created intelligence.

Read Rev. 21: 10–18.

"And he carried me away in the spirit to a great and high mountain, and showed me that great city, the holy Jerusalem, descending out of heaven from God: having the glory of God: and her light was like unto a stone most precious, even like a jasper stone, clear as crystal: and had a wall great and high, and had twelve gates, and at the gates twelve angels, and names written thereon, which are the names of the twelve tribes of the children of Israel: on the east three gates; on the north three gates; on the south three gates; and on the west three gates. And the wall of the city had twelve foundations, and in them the names of the twelve apostles of the Lamb. And he that talked with me had a golden reed to measure the city, and the gates thereof, and the wall thereof. And the city lieth foursquare, and the length is as large as the breadth: and he measured the city with the reed, twelve thousand furlongs. The length and the breadth and the height of it are equal. And he measured the wall thereof, a hundred and forty and four cubits, according to the measure of a man, that is, of the angel. And the building of the wall of it was of jasper: and the city was pure gold, like unto clear glass."

Supt. Further description will be given by members of the BIBLE CLASS; first, as to the foundations of the wall of the city.

First Bible Class Pupil. 'And the foundations of the wall of the city were garnished with all manner of precious stones. The first foundation was jasper; the second, sapphire; the third, a chalcedony; the fourth, an emerald; the fifth, sardonyx; the sixth, sardius; the seventh, chrysolite; the eighth, beryl; the ninth, a topaz: the tenth, a chrysoprasus; the eleventh, a jacinth: the twelfth, an amethyst."—Rev. 21. 19–20.

Supt. Second, as to the gates and streets?

Second Bible Class Pupil. "And the twelve gates were twelve pearls; every several gate was of one pearl: and the street of the city was pure gold, as it were transparent glass."—Rev. 21: 21.

Supt. Third, as to the light of the city?

Third Bible Class Pupil. "And the city had no need of the sun, neither of the moon, to shine in it: for the glory of God did lighten it, and the Lamb is the light thereof."—Rev. 21: 23.

Supt. What of the river of the city?

Fourth Bible Class Pupil. "And he showed me a pure river of water of life, clear as crystal, proceeding out of the throne of God and of the Lamb."— Rev. 22 : 1.

Supt. What of the tree of life?

Fifth Bible Class Pupil. "In the midst of the street of it, and on either side of the river, was there the tree of life, which bare twelve manner of fruits, and yielded her fruit every month: and the leaves of the tree were for the healing of the nations."— Rev. 22 : 2.

Supt. As to the government of this holy city?

Sixth Bible Class Pupil. "And there shall be no more curse: but the throne of God and of the Lamb shall be in it; and his servants shall serve him: and they shall see his face; and his name shall be in their foreheads."— Rev. 22 : 3, 4.

Supt. How are we invited to those mansions of light in this glorious city?

Seventh Bible Class Pupil. "I, Jesus, have sent mine angel to testify unto you these things in the churches. I am the root and the offspring of David, and the bright and morning star. And the Spirit and the bride say, Come. And let him that heareth say, Come. And let him that is athirst come. And whosoever will, let him take the water of life freely."— Rev. 22 : 16, 17.

Supt. Is there danger in rejecting the precious invitation?

Eighth Bible Class Pupil. "Blessed are they that do his commandments, that they may have right to the tree of life, and may enter in through the gates into the city. For without are dogs, and sorcerers, and whoremongers, and murderers, and idolaters, and whosoever loveth and maketh a lie."—Rev. 22 : 14, 15.

Supt. Is there a time beyond which to reject the offers of mercy is to reject them forever?

"And he saith unto me, Seal not the sayings of the prophecy of this book: for the time is at hand. He that is unjust, let him be unjust still: and he which is filthy, let him be filthy still: and he that is righteous, let him be righteous still: and he that is holy, let him be holy still. And, behold, I come quickly; and my reward is with me, to give every man according as his work shall be."—Rev. 22: 10, 11, 12.

Song. "Jerusalem the Golden," the song of the Celestial Country.—Fresh Laurels, p. 87. Or, "Beautiful Zion, built above."—Happy Voices, p. 214.

CLOSING PART.

(*By a Class of Teachers.*)

Supt. What shall be our lot and place if we gain admission to the New Jerusalem?

First Teacher. We shall be made pillars in the temple of our God.

"Him that overcometh will I make a pillar in the temple of my God, and he shall go no more out."—Rev. 3: 12.

Supt. What does this promise mean?

Same Teacher. It means that the victorious Christian shall have the honor to be an important and useful part in the society of heaven.

Second Teacher. We shall go no more out forever.

"Him that overcometh will I make a pillar in the temple of my God, and he shall go no more out."—Rev. 3: 12.

This is one of the most precious of the promises. Once within those pearly gates and we shall be from sin and death forever secure.

Third Teacher. We shall inherit all things.

"He that overcometh shall inherit all things; and I will be his God, and he shall be my son."—Rev. 21: 7.

All the priceless treasures of that princely realm shall be ours, the free gift of him who has begotten us, "To an inheritance incorruptible, and undefiled, and that fadeth not away."

Fourth Teacher. We shall have seen the end of all suffering and sorrow.

"They shall hunger no more, neither thirst any more; neither shall the sun light on them, nor any heat: for the Lamb which is in the midst of the throne shall feed them, and shall lead them unto living fountains of waters: and God shall wipe away all tears from their eyes."—Rev. 7: 16, 17.

Fifth Teacher. "And I will write upon him the name of my God, and the name of the city of my God, which is New Jerusalem, which cometh down out of heaven from my God: and I will write upon him my new name."

This the most glorious of all, the very culmination of the Saviour's promises. Divine love could go no farther. This indeed is to be *lost in Christ.*

BRIEF ADDRESS,

Concerning the worth of this inheritance which all may attain.

CLOSING HYMN.

Heaven is my home.

APPENDIX.

THE

GENERAL EXERCISES,

THEIR CHARACTER AND IMPORTANCE.

How to conduct the devotions of the School and Concert Service has often proved a hard question.

The Sunday School is a place of worship as well as of study. Its exercises should be devotional as well as instructive. The young heart is to be won to Christ and trained for heaven, as well as the mind enlightened, by the Word of Truth and the Spirit of God.

PRAYER.

The prayer of the school, uttered by the voice of the Superintendent, should be the offering of every heart. Let its language be simple, its sentences short, its expression of supplication that which every little heart can offer for daily want and present need, its ascriptions of praise and thanksgiving such as every little mind can understand and every soul feel.

READING.

In very manner as well as in matter the reading in the Sunday School should not only be impressive, but such as to awaken the spirit of true devotion. It should be varied, sometimes by the Superintendent alone, at other times by the Superintendent and school responsively. The Superintendent should always make special preparation for the reading, no matter how familiar the selection may be. He should be able to read with his eyes principally upon the school, and always have so much of the spirit of the words in his own heart as to be able to inspire his hearers with the same spirit.

SINGING, ETC.

No part of the Sunday School exercise is more important than the music. We cannot overrate the power of song. Let us not fail to have this mighty power well directed. I know not which most to deprecate in our Sunday School songs — unsuitable words or improper music. Mr. Eggleston says, in his Sunday School Manual,* "Do not sing anything merely for the excitement of the tune. There may be some apology for this sort of singing when it is intended to wake up the flagging spirits of small children. But even then, why not sing something that has sense and devotion in it, instead of such an one as 'My Sabbath Song,' or 'We are Young and We are Happy?' Above all, do not neglect the grand old church hymns, but sing such of them as are full of life and power."

An adult congregation can play mock attention, but children need to understand what is said or sung to be interested. I remember the evident dissatisfaction of a little girl who turned to her teacher with the honest inquiry: "What does all this mean?" after singing through the following words of one of our popular Sunday School songs: "O! Golden

*Note.— The Sunday School Manual, by Edward Eggleston, D. D., published by Adams, Blackmer, & Lyon, should be in the hands of every Sunday School teacher who aspires to a high degree of usefulness.

hereafter, Thine every bright rafter will shake with the thunder of sanctified song; O! chorus of fire, that will burst from God's choir," etc.

Much that is printed in verse for Sunday School recitation and singing is unworthy the name of poetry. Our Sunday School literature should be rid of all this. The literature of the Bible may be our standard. There is no *religious doggerel* or meaningless grand eloquence either in the Old or New Testaments.

Let us strive to elevate the minds and cultivate the tastes of our children by presenting to them the real and the true, as well as the good and the beautiful.

In the Sunday School service let us sing and do all that we do with the spirit and the understanding also.

A few selections are given in this closing chapter for recitations, responsive reading, chanting, etc. From these and others of like character selections can be made to render the service of the school and concert varied and impressive.

SELECTIONS,

RESPONSIVE READINGS, CHANTS, ETC.

I.—SELECTIONS.

AN OPENING EXERCISE.

Superintendent. "The Lord is in his holy temple. Let all the earth keep silence before him."—Hab. 2 : 20.

"Thou shalt love the Lord thy God with all thine heart, and with all thy soul, and with all thy might. And these words which I command thee this day shall be in thine heart. And thou shalt teach them diligently unto the children, and shalt talk of them when thou sittest in thine house, and when thou walkest by the way, and when thou liest down, and when thou risest up."—Deut. 6 : 5–7.

"And thou shalt teach them ordinances and laws, and shalt show them the way wherein they must walk, and the work that they must do."—Ex. 18 : 20

Teachers' response (rising). "Let the words of my mouth, and the meditation of my heart, be acceptable in thy sight, O Lord, my strength and my Redeemer."—Ps. 19: 14.

"The law of the Lord is perfect, converting the soul; the testimony of the Lord is sure, making wise the simple; the statutes of the Lord are right, rejoicing the heart; the commandment of the Lord is pure, enlightening the eyes."—Ps. 19: 7, 8.

"Come and hear, all ye that fear God, and I will declare what he hath done for my soul."

Children's response (rising). "Show me thy ways, O Lord; teach me thy paths. Lead me in thy truth and teach me."—Ps. 25: 4, 5.

"Teach me thy way, O Lord; I will walk in thy truth."—Psalm 86: 11.

"The mercy of the Lord is from everlasting to everlasting,"

Supt. "Upon them that fear him,"—Ps. 103: 17.

Children. "And his righteousness unto children's children,'

Teachers. "To such as keep his covenant, and to those that remember his commandments to do them."—Ps. 103: 18.

All recite. "Jesus said, Suffer little children, and forbid them not, to come unto me: for of such is the kingdom of heaven."

A PRAYER.

1 Father, I have wandered far,
Oh! be now my guiding star!
Draw my footsteps back to thee,
Set my struggling spirit free;
Save me from the doubts that roll
O'er the chaos of my soul—
Let one ray of truth illume
And dispel the thickening gloom!
God of truth, and peace, and love,
Hear my prayer!
Drive my restless thoughts above,
Keep them there!

2 Father, save me at this hour
From the tempter's fearful power,
Purify the hidden springs
Of my wild imaginings:
I have thought, till thought is pain,
Searched for peace, till search is vain;
Out of *thee*, I cannot find
Rest for the immortal mind.
Now I come to thee for aid—
Peace restore!
Let my soul on thee be stayed
For evermore!

GO WHEN THE MORNING SHINETH.

1 Go when the morning shineth,
Go when the noon is bright,
Go when the eve declineth,
Go in the hush of night,
Go with pure mind and feeling,
Fling earthly thought away,
And, in thy closet kneeling,
Do thou in secret pray.

2 Oh, not a joy or blessing
With this can we compare—
The grace our Father gave us
To pour our souls in prayer:
Whene'er thou pin'st in sadness,
Before his footstool fall;
Remember, in thy gladness,
His love who gave thee all.

3 Remember all who love thee,
All who are loved by thee;
Pray, too, for those who hate thee,
If any such there be;
Then for thyself, in meekness,
A blessing humbly claim,
And blend with each petition
Thy great Redeemer's name.

THE TWENTY-THIRD PSALM.

1 The Lord is my Shepherd, and I am his lamb,
One of the smallest and frailest I am,
Yet, by his bounty daily I'm fed,
In his green pastures tenderly led.

2 Kind is my Shepherd, and large is the fold
To which he calleth the young as the old,
Tenderly watching in waking and sleep,
Over us, evermore, guard he doth keep.

3 Sometimes, the way where he leadeth his sheep
Grows for my child-feet, dark and too steep;
Then doth he lift me up close to his breast,
Bearing me upward to places of rest.

4 When I had wandered away from his side,
Into the path which the sinning have tried,
He, o'er each step of sin's rugged track,
Patiently, lovingly, guided me back.

5 He hath green pastures — lying afar —
Needing no sunlight, needing no star —
There, from his presence, the lambs *never* stray;
Thither, he leadeth me — nearer each day.

6 But closer than meadows brightened by faith,
Lieth the valley of silence and death;
Seeing its shadows — yet fearless I am,
For the Lord is my Shepherd, and I am his lamb!

—*Mary Lowe.*

LOVING SHEPHERD.

1 Loving Shepherd, kind and true,
  Wilt thou not in pity come
To thy lamb? as shepherds do,
  Bear me in thy bosom home;
Take me hence from earth's annoy
To thy home of endless joy?

2 See how I have gone astray
  In this earthly wilderness;
Come and take me hence away
  To thy flock who dwell in bliss,
And thy glory, Lord, behold,
Safe within thy heavenly fold.

3 Here I live in sore distress,
  Careful, timid, every hour;
For my foes around me press,
  Hem me in with craft and power:
Not one moment safe can be,
Lord, thy lamb, away from thee.

4 O Lord Jesus, let me not
  'Mid the ravening wolves e'er fall;
Help me as a shepherd ought,
  That I may escape them all:
Bear me homeward in thy breast
To thy fold of endless rest.

—*Angelus, 1657.*

THE LORD WILL PROVIDE.

(Adapted to Concert Exercise, "Abraham: a Lesson of Faith.")

1 In some way or other the Lord will provide;
It may not be *my* way,
It may not be *thy* way,
And yet, in his *own* way,
The Lord will provide.

2 At some time or other the Lord will provide;
It may not be *my* time,
It may not be *thy* time,
And yet, in his *own* time,
The Lord will provide.

3 Despond then no longer, the Lord will provide;
And this be the token:
No word he hath spoken
Was ever yet broken;
The Lord will provide.

4 March on then right boldly; the sea shall divide,
The pathway made glorious;
With shoutings victorious,
We'll join in the chorus
The Lord will provide.

HOW CAN A CHILD BE SAVED?

1 How can a child be saved,
His sins be all forgiven?
How may he, on his dying day,
Stand at the gate of heaven?

2 He must repent, with all his heart,
And strive to serve his God,
In simple faith he must rely
On Christ's atoning blood.

3 Through that alone is welcome found
At yonder pearly gate;
Thousands have entered young as we,
Nor shall we lingering wait.

"THE OPEN GATE."

1 Mercy, with her wings unfolded,
Bending o'er her children dear,
Softly whispers "Come to Jesus,"
How he loves your praise to hear.

2 With his gracious arms extended,
See the kind Redeemer wait;
Now he folds the lambs that enter,
Joyful through the open gate.

3 Shall we cling to earthly pleasures,
When the shining angels wait,
Calling children to the Saviour,
Standing at the open gate?

THE OLD, OLD STORY.

(Appropriate to the Exercise for Christmas.)

1 Tell me the old, old story,
Of unseen things above,—
Of Jesus and his glory,
Of Jesus and his love.

2 Tell me the story simply,
As to a little child;
For I am weak and weary,
And helpless and defiled.

3 Tell me the story slowly,
That I may take it in—
That wonderful redemption,
God's remedy for sin.

4 Tell me the story often,
For I forget so soon;
The early dew of morning
Has passed away at noon.

5 Tell me the story softly,
With earnest tones and grave;
Remember, *I'm* the sinner
Whom Jesus came to save.

6 Tell me the story always,
If you would really be
In any time of trouble,
A comforter to me.

7 Tell me the same old story,
When you have cause to fear
That this world's empty glory
Is costing me too dear.

8 Yes, and when that world's glory
Shall dawn upon my soul,
Tell me the old, old story,
"Christ Jesus makes thee whole."

THE CROSS PRESENTED.

There is no other way unto life, and unto true inward peace, than the way of the holy cross and of daily self-denial.

Christ's whole life was a cross and a martyrdom; and dost thou seek rest and enjoyment for thyself?

Let thyself therefore, like a good and faithful servant of Christ, bear manfully the cross of thy Lord, who out of love was crucified for thee.

Drink of the Lord's cup with hearty affection, if thou desire to be his friend, and to have part with him.— *Thomas a Kempis.*

THE WAY OF THE CROSS, THE WAY OF LIGHT.

(Appropriate to the Exercise, " The Cross and the Crown.")

1 Through the cross comes the crown; when the cares of this life,
Like giants in strength, may to crush thee combine,
Never mind, never mind! after sorrow's sad strife
Shall the peace and the crown of salvation be thine.

2 Through woe comes delight; if at evening thou sigh,
And thy soul still at midnight in sorrow appears,
Never mind, never mind! for the morning is nigh,
Whose sunbeams of gladness shall dry up thy tears!

3 Through death comes our life; to the portal of pain,
Through Time's thistle-fields are our weary steps driven,
Never mind, never mind! through this passage we gain
The mansions of light and the portals of heaven.

—*From the German.*

THE SEA OF GALILEE.

(Adapted to Concert Exercise, "Around Gennesaret.")

How pleasant to me thy deep blue wave,
O sea of Galilee!
For the glorious One who came to save,
Hath often stood by thee.
Fair are the lakes in the land I love,
Where pine and heather grow,
But thou hast loveliness above
What nature can bestow.
It is not that the wild gazelle
Comes down to drink thy tide
But he that was pierced to save from hell
Oft wandered by thy side.
Graceful around thee, the mountains meet,
Thou calm reposing sea;
But ah! far more the beautiful feet
Of Jesus walked o'er thee.
Those days are past — Bethsaida where,
Chorazin where art thou?
His tent the wild Arab pitches there,
The wild reeds shade thy brow.
Tell me ye mouldering fragments, tell,
Was the Saviour's city here?
Lifted to heaven, has it sunk to hell,
With none to shed a tear?
O Saviour! gone to God's right hand,
Yet the same Saviour still,
Graved on thy heart is this lovely strand
And every fragrant hill.

JERUSALEM THE GOLDEN.

1 Jerusalem, the golden,
I languish for one gleam
Of all thy glory, folden
In distance and in dream.
My thoughts, like palms in exile
Climb up to look, and pray
For a glimpse of that dear country
That lies so far away.

2 Jerusalem, the golden,
  There all our birds that flew,
Our flowers but half unfolden,
  Our pearls that turned to dew,
And all the glad life-music,
  Now heard no longer here,
Shall come again to greet us
  As we are drawing near.

3 Jerusalem, the golden,
  I toil on, day by day;
Heartsore, each night with longing,
  I stretch my hands and pray
That 'midst the leaves of healing
  My soul may find her rest,
Where the wicked cease from troubling,
  And the weary are at rest.

BEAUTIFUL THINGS ABOVE.

1 There's a beautiful *river* above,
  Which flows from the midst of the throne,
Whose surface no tempests disturb;
  Unruffled it sweetly flows on.

2 There's a beautiful *city* above,
  With walls decked with jewels so rare,
With streets of pure, bright, shining gold,
  With which nothing on earth may compare.

3 There are beautiful *mansions* above,
  Prepared by the Saviour for those
Who look for salvation to him,
  And on himself only repose.

4 There's a beautiful *anthem* above
  Which the glorified ever shall sing,
Whose notes as they swell through the heavens,
  Sweet praise to the Saviour shall bring.

5 There are beautiful *angels* above
  Surrounding the throne of the Lamb,
Whose service — blest service — it is
  To worship, unceasing, his name.

6 And *all* these bright, beautiful things,
  And more than the heart can conceive
Are offered by God in his love
  To all who on Jesus believe.

THE QUEEN'S DECISION.

(Adapted to Concert Exercise, "The Name of Jesus.")

Once upon a time, long ago, the Queen of Language sent forth a proclamation that on such a day there would be a convention of all classes of people, who might take her trusty servants, the alphabet, consisting of twenty-four letters, and the one who should form the sweetest word should be seated next to the Queen and receive a crown of gold.

Far and wide the proclamation went, and multitudes began to study what word they would form. But lest somebody else should select his chosen word, every one kept silent and only looked wise, as much as to say: "I know something, if I only chose to tell."

At length the day arrived, and there was the Queen, and there the crown and the alphabet, and all the multitude. The question now was, who should first spell what he considered the most beautiful word in the world. So the Queen told them all to carefully write their word, and fold it up, and cast it into a box which she had prepared. She would then draw them out by lot, read the word aloud, call upon the writer to stand up, and she would then decide upon each. So she drew all the multitude close around her, and all were hushed and silent, when she put in her hand and drew out a paper. On opening it, she read aloud "MONEY!"

"Whose is this?" asked the Queen.

"It is mine," said an old hard-faced miser.

"And why do you think this the sweetest word in the human language?" she said.

"Because, madam, money is what all want, all toil for, and all rejoice over. It will buy anything, do anything, and, as the good book says, 'money answereth all things.' It is the sweetest word ever spoken."

"I beg leave to differ from you, sir. You pervert the meaning of the good book. You say money will do anything, and procure anything. Is that so? Will it raise the sick man from a bed of pain? Will it cheer or save the dying man? Will it heal a wounded conscience? Will it restore the dead babe to its mother's arms? Will it open the door of heaven to the soul, or make immortality blessed? No! It is a slippery servant to minister to the wants of the body, or to raise the pride, or to pamper the appetites, or a hard master to grind the poor. It is anything but the sweetest word."

She then put her hand again into the box and drew out a paper, on which was written the word "HONOR."

"Who claims this?"

"I do," said a fine-looking young man, dressed in splendid military garments.

"And what is your plea for your favorite word?" said the Queen.

"Why, madam, it seems to me too plain for argument. The child at school, the boy on the play-ground, the parent in planning for his child, the scholar in wasting life over his books, the sailor in risking his life on the stormy ocean, the politician in wrestling for position, and the soldier rushing up to the cannon's mouth, all are witnesses that *honor* is the word, above all others, that is sweetest to the human ear."

"You plead well," said the Queen, "but I cannot agree with you. Honor is a powerful instrument with which to move men to effort and action. But you will notice that it appeals to and cultivates supreme selfishness in the heart, shuts out domestic affections, tramples on the most sacred rights of others, seeks its place through fields of blood, and often fills nations with wailing. I cannot allow you the premium, sir."

Again the fair hand of the Queen drew from the box, and on the paper was written the word "LOVE."

"Whose may this be?" asked the Queen in a softened voice.

"Mine, madam," said a young man, whose face was glowing with excitement, while a thousand youths around him, and as many bright-eyed maidens, seemed ready to shout.

"And your reasons, sir?"

"It is not a matter of reason, madam, but it is the verdict of the mother over her babe, of that babe as soon as he can return her smile, of the child longing for home, of the widow in her desolation, of youth seeking the dearest friend the earth knows, of age leaning upon the child for support. It is sung in the songs of the birds, echoed in the notes of the mourning dove, and it thrills in the language of every living thing. We have reason to believe that it reaches the angels of heaven."

"A strong plea certainly," said the Queen; "but I must have time to think further upon it before I decide."

Once more she drew from the box, and the word was read amid great silence, "JESUS."

"Whose is this?" said the Queen, in a low, soft tone.

"I wrote it," said a sweet little girl, almost sinking under the eyes that were turned upon her.

"And can you, my child, tell me the reasons why you think JESUS the sweetest word in the world?"

"No; I only feel so."

"Truly, little one, you feel right. There is no attribute of humanity, no beauty of character, no greatness in our idea, nothing exalted, refined, gentle, loving, or good, which is not found in him. He is riches, and honor, and glory, and love in its deepest meaning. There has been no language found on earth, into which JESUS cannot be introduced, untranslated. The Jew, the Greek, the Hottentot, and the refined nations of the earth all sing the same name. It *is* the sweetest word on earth, and probably the sweetest in heaven! Come, little child, and sit by my side and receive this golden crown—faint emblem of the crown which Jesus will one day place upon thy head!"—*Rev. John Todd, from Nat. S. S. Teacher.*

THE MOUNTAINS OF THE BIBLE.

1 Beautiful mountains that point us to heaven,
Showing the love that to mortals is given,
Teaching us truly the way we should go;
Resting, believing, obeying below,
Praying, repenting, and happy alway—
These are the lessons ye teach us to-day.

2 Mountain of rest, where the waters were stayed,
Mountains of refuge, where Israel strayed,
When in our weary way all tempest tossed,
Each cherished hope we had seen to be lost;
Then, on Mount Ararat, see we with joy,
His bow of beauty "I will not destroy."

3 Mountain of promise, "the Lord will provide,"
Abram with Isaac and God glorified;
Mountain of worship, where thousands of feet
Hasted to offer their incense so sweet;
Doubting and daring God's ways to impeach,
Sweet are the lessons Moriah will teach.

4 Mountain of conflict, where David prevailed,
Where mocking Jebusites signally failed;
In all our strivings with error and sin,
Foes from without and the foes from within,
How glad we hear, "As Mount Zion shall be,
They that trust in the Lord," he maketh free.

5 Mountain of prayer, where the Saviour could say
"Father, thy will, not mine own," I obey;
Here may we learn all our burdens to bear,
Here lighten sorrows and lessen our care;
All in the dark we to Olivet go,
But heaven's own light will our Father bestow.

6 Mountain of sacrifice, solemn and grand!
Penitent must all at Calvary stand;
God in his holiness dying for sin,
Opens the portals that sinners pass in,
Takes all our guilt away, makes us his own;
Oh, shall such love as this vainly atone?

7 Mountain immortal to poor human need,
Hermon, that tells of "Christ risen indeed;"
Dying, he lives, and his children shall live
Amid all the bliss that his heaven can give;
Ah, we can bear all the woes of this now
In hope of glories, that circle thy brow.

8 O sacred mountains, while here we may stay,
Oft to thy summits our willing feet stray,
Ararat whispers of rest, sweet and true,
On Mount Moriah our faith we renew;
Zion forbids, that in conflict we fail,
Olivet makes all our prayers to prevail;
Calvary gives us a Saviour so fond,
Hermon a glimpse of the glory beyond;
Beautiful mountains, ye teach us to-day,
Christ is our all in all now and for aye.

Mrs. Wm. J. Smith.

OUR WORK IS HERE.

No crown awaits us but that for which we've borne a cross.

1 We must either meet or miss him,
  As we pass from earth away;
We shall either gain or lose him,
  In this tenement of clay;
For 'tis here his work lies open,
  Not in heaven — the crown is there;
Earth the cross holds, which for Jesus
  We must without murmuring bear.

2 We must wait, and watch, and labor,
  Striving well Christ's work to do;
Tending e'er our journey heavenward,
  Treading every footstep true;
Bearing well each other's burdens,
  Leaving treasures on the way;
Scattering golden life *immortelles*
  That will never fade away.

3 Let us onward then for Jesus,
  Let us gird his armor on;
Ever praying, as we're marching,
  That "his will alone be done."
Then we will not miss our Saviour,
  But we'll meet him on the way,
As we pass to yonder mansion
  Where the heavenly sunbeams play.

G—— N——.

II.—RESPONSIVE READINGS.

PSALM I.

1 Blessed is the man that walketh not in the counsel of the ungodly,
Nor standeth in the way of sinners,
Nor sitteth in the seat of the scornful.
2 But his delight is in the law of the Lord;
And in his law doth he meditate day and night.

3 And he shall be like a tree planted by the rivers of water,
That bringeth forth his fruit in his season;
His leaf also shall not wither;
And whatsoever he doeth shall prosper.
4 The ungodly are not so:
But are like the chaff which the wind driveth away.
5 Therefore the ungodly shall not stand in the judgment,
Nor sinners in the congregation of the righteous.
6 For the Lord knoweth the way of the righteous:
But the way of the ungodly shall perish.

PSALM VIII.

1 O Lord, our Lord,
How excellent is thy name in all the earth!
Who hast set thy glory above the heavens.
2 Out of the mouth of babes and sucklings hast thou ordained strength,
Because of thine enemies,
That thou mightest still the enemy and the avenger.
3 When I consider thy heavens, the work of thy fingers,
The moon and the stars, which thou hast ordained;
4 What is man, that thou art mindful of him?
And the son of man, that thou visitest him?
5 For thou hast made him a little lower than the angels,
And hast crowned him with glory and honor.
6 Thou madest him to have dominion over the works of thy hands;
Thou hast put all things under his feet:
7 All sheep and oxen,
Yea, and the beasts of the field;
8 The fowl of the air, and the fish of the sea,
And whatsoever passeth through the paths of the seas.
9 O Lord, our Lord,
How excellent is thy name in all the earth!

PSALM XXIV.

1 The earth is the Lord's, and the fullness thereof;
The world, and they that dwell therein.

2 For he hath founded it upon the seas,
And established it upon the floods.

3 Who shall ascend into the hill of the Lord?
And who shall stand in his holy place?

4 He that hath clean hands, and a pure heart;
Who hath not lifted up his soul unto vanity,
Nor sworn deceitfully.

5 He shall receive the blessing from the Lord,
And righteousness from the God of his salvation.

6 This is the generation of them that seek him,
That seek thy face, O Jacob.

7 Lift up your heads, O ye gates;
And be ye lifted up, ye everlasting doors;
And the King of Glory shall come in.

8 Who is this King of Glory?
The Lord strong and mighty; the Lord mighty in battle.

9 Lift up your heads, O ye gates; even lift them up, ye everlasting doors;
And the King of Glory shall come in.

10 Who is this King of Glory?
The Lord of Hosts, he is the King of Glory.

PSALM XC.

1 Lord, thou hast been our dwelling place,
In all generations.

2 Before the mountains were brought forth,
Or ever thou hadst formed the earth and the world,
Even from everlasting to everlasting, thou art God.

3 Thou turnest man to destruction;
And sayest, Return, ye children of men.

4 For a thousand years in thy sight are but as yesterday when it is past,
And as a watch in the night.

5 Thou carriest them away as with a flood; they are as a sleep:
In the morning they are like grass which groweth up;

6 In the morning it flourisheth, and groweth up,
In the evening it is cut down, and withereth.

7 For we are consumed by thine anger,
And by thy wrath we are troubled.

8 Thou hast set our iniquities before thee,
Our secret sins in the light of thy countenance.

9 For all our days are passed away in thy wrath:
We spend our years as a tale that is told.

10 The days of our years are threescore years and ten;
And if by reason of strength they be fourscore years,
Yet is their strength labour and sorrow;
For it is soon cut off, and we fly away.

11 Who knoweth the power of thine anger?
Even according to thy fear, so is thy wrath.

12 So teach us to number our days,
That we may apply our hearts unto wisdom.

13 Return, O Lord, how long?
And let it repent thee concerning thy servants.

14 O satisfy us early with thy mercy;
That we may rejoice and be glad all our days.

15 Make us glad according to the days wherein thou hast afflicted us,
And the years wherein we have seen evil.

16 Let thy work appear unto thy servants,
And thy glory unto their children.

17 And let the beauty of the Lord our God be upon us:
And establish thou the work of our hands upon us;
YEA, THE WORK OF OUR HANDS ESTABLISH THOU IT.

PSALM CIII.

1 Bless the Lord, O my soul:
And all that is within me, bless his holy name.

2 Bless the Lord, O my soul,
And forget not all his benefits:

3 Who forgiveth all thine iniquities;
Who healeth all thy diseases;

4 Who redeemeth thy life from destruction;
Who crowneth thee with lovingkindness and tender mercies;

5 Who satisfieth thy mouth with good things;
So that thy youth is renewed like the eagle's.

6 The Lord executeth righteousness,
And judgment for all that are oppressed.

7 He made known his ways unto Moses,
His acts unto the children of Israel.

8 The Lord is merciful and gracious,
Slow to anger and plenteous in mercy.

9 He will not always chide:
Neither will he keep his anger for ever.

10 He hath not dealt with us after our sins;
Nor rewarded us according to our iniquities

11 For as the heaven is high above the earth,
So great is his mercy toward them that fear him.

12 As far as the east is from the west,
So far hath he removed our transgressions from us.

13 Like as a father pitieth his children,
So the Lord pitieth them that fear him.

14 For he knoweth our frame;
He remembereth that we are dust.

15 As for man, his days are as grass:
As a flower of the field, so he flourisheth.

16 For the wind passeth over it, and it is gone;
And the place thereof shall know it no more.

17 But the mercy of the Lord is from everlasting to everlasting upon them that fear him.

PSALM CXIX. 97–105.

97 Oh how love I thy law!
It is my meditation all the day.

98 Thou through thy commandments hast made me wiser than mine enemies:
For they are ever with me.

99 I have more understanding than all my teachers:
For thy testimonies are my meditation.

100 I understand more than the ancients,
Because I keep thy precepts.

101 I have refrained my feet from every evil way,
That I might keep thy word.

102 I have not departed from thy judgments,
For thou hast taught me.

103 How sweet are thy words unto my taste!
Yea, sweeter than honey to my mouth.

104 Through thy precepts I get understanding:
Therefore I hate every false way.

105 Thy word is a lamp unto my feet,
And a light unto my path.

PSALM CXXV.

1 They that trust in the Lord shall be as Mount Zion,
Which cannot be removed, but abideth for ever.

2 As the mountains are round about Jerusalem,
So the Lord is round about his people, from henceforth even for ever.

3 For the rod of the wicked shall not rest upon the lot of the righteous;
Lest the righteous put forth their hands unto iniquity.

4 Do good, O Lord, unto those that be good,
And to them that are upright in their hearts.

5 As for such as turn aside unto their crooked ways,
The Lord shall lead them forth with the workers of iniquity:
BUT PEACE SHALL BE UPON ISRAEL.

ISAIAH XI. 1–9.

1 And there shall come forth a rod out of the stem of Jesse,
And a branch shall grow out of his roots:

2 And the Spirit of the Lord shall rest upon him,
The spirit of wisdom and understanding,
The spirit of counsel and might,
The spirit of knowledge and of the fear of the Lord;

3 And shall make him of quick understanding,
In the fear of the Lord:
And he shall not judge after the sight of his eyes,
Neither reprove after the hearing of his ears:

4 But with righteousness shall he judge the poor,
And reprove with equity for the meek of the earth.
And he shall smite the earth with the rod of his mouth,
And with the breath of his lips shall he slay the wicked.
5 And righteousness shall be the girdle of his loins,
And faithfulness the girdle of his reins.
6 The wolf also shall dwell with the lamb,
And the leopard shall lie down with the kid;
And the calf, and the young lion, and the fatling together;
And a little child shall lead them.
7 And the cow and the bear shall feed; their young ones shall lie down together;
And the lion shall eat straw like the ox.
8 And the sucking child shall play on the hole of the asp,
And the weaned child shall put his hand on the cockatrice' den.
9 They shall not hurt nor destroy in all my holy mountain;
For the earth shall be full of the knowledge of the Lord, as the waters cover the sea.

ISAIAH LV. 1–7.

1 Ho, every one that thirsteth, come ye to the waters,
And he that hath no money; come ye, buy and eat;
Yea, come, buy wine and milk,
Without money and without price.
2 Wherefore do ye spend money for that which is not bread?
And your labor for that which satisfieth not?
Hearken diligently unto me, and eat ye that which is good,
And let your soul delight itself in fatness.
3 Incline your ear, and come unto me;
Hear, and your soul shall live:
And I will make an everlasting covenant with you,
Even the sure mercies of David.
4 Behold, I have given him for a witness to the people,
A leader and commander to the people.
5 Behold, thou shalt call a nation that thou knowest not,
And nations that knew not thee shall run unto thee,

Because of the Lord thy God, and for the Holy One of Israel;
For he hath glorified thee.

6 Seek ye the Lord while he may be found,
Call ye upon him while he is near:

7 Let the wicked forsake his way,
And the unrighteous man his thoughts:

And let him return unto the Lord, and he will have mercy upon him;
And to our God, for he will abundantly pardon.

THE BEATITUDES.

1 And seeing the multitudes, he went up into a mountain: and when he was set, his disciples came unto him:

2 And he opened his mouth, and taught them, saying,

3 Blessed are the poor in spirit: for theirs is the kingdom of heaven.

4 Blessed are they that mourn: for they shall be comforted.

5 Blessed are the meek: for they shall inherit the earth.

6 Blessed are they which do hunger and thirst after righteousness: for they shall be filled.

7 Blessed are the merciful: for they shall obtain mercy.

8 Blessed are the pure in heart: for they shall see God.

9 Blessed are the peacemakers: for they shall be called the children of God.

10 Blessed are they which are persecuted for righteousness' sake: for theirs is the kingdom of heaven.

11 Blessed are ye, when men shall revile you, and persecute you. and shall say all manner of evil against you falsely, for my sake.

12 Rejoice, and be exceeding glad: for great is your reward in heaven: for so persecuted they the prophets which were before you.

THE APOSTLES' CREED.

I BELIEVE in GOD, the FATHER Almighty, Maker of heaven and earth:

And in JESUS CHRIST his only Son our Lord; Who was conceived by the HOLY GHOST, Born of the Virgin Mary, Suffered under Pontius Pilate, Was crucified, dead, and buried; He descended into hell; [i. e. continued under the power of death.] The third day he rose from the dead; He ascended into heaven, And sitteth on the right hand of GOD the Father Almighty; From thence he shall come to judge both the quick and the dead.

I believe in the HOLY GHOST; The Holy Catholic Church; The Communion of Saints; The Forgiveness of sins; The Resurrection of the body, And the Life everlasting. Amen.

III.—CHANTS, ETC.

THE LORD'S PRAYER.

(To either of the foregoing chants.)

1 Our Father, who art in heaven, hallowed | be Thy | name.
Thy kingdom come. Thy will be done, on | earth ·· as it | is in | heaven.

2 Give us this day our | dai-ly | bread.
And forgive us our trespasses, as we forgive | them that | trespass ·· a- | gainst us.

3 And lead us not into temptation; but deliver | us from | evil:
For Thine is the kingdom, and the power, and the glory, for- | e-ver. | A— | men.

THE SAVIOUR.

1 And Jesus said, Suffer little children, and forbid them not to | come ·· unto | me;
For of | such ·· is the | kingdom ·· of | heaven.

2 He shall feed his | flock ·· like a | shepherd:
He shall gather the lambs with his arm and | carry ·· them | in his | bosom.

3 I will pour my Spirit upon thy seed, and my blessing up- | on thine | offspring;
And they shall spring up as among the grass, as | willows ·· by the | wa-ter- | courses.

GLORIA PATRI.

Glory be to the Father, and | to the | Son, ‖ and | to the | Ho-ly | Ghost;

As it was in the beginning, is now, and | ever ·· shall | be, ‖ world | with-out | end. A- | men.

No. 3.

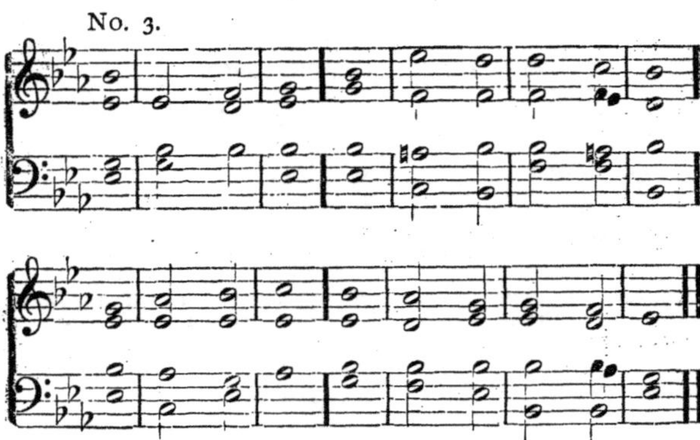

PSALM XCVIII.

1 Oh sing unto the | Lord ·· a new | song; ‖ for he | hath done | marvel-ous | things.

2 With his own right hand, and with his | ho-ly | arm, ‖ hath he | gotten ·· him- | self the | victory.

3 The Lord declared | his sal- | vation; ‖ his righteousness hath he openly showed | in the | sight ·· of the | heathen.

4 He hath remembered his mercy and truth toward the | house of | Israel; ‖ and all the ends of the world have seen the sal- | va-tion | of our | God.

5 Show yourselves joyful unto the Lord, | all ye | lands. ‖ sing, re- | joice, and | give— | thanks.

6 Praise the Lord up- | on the | harp; ‖ sing to the harp with a | psalm of | thanks— | giving.

7 With trumpets, | also, ·· and | shawms, ‖ Oh show yourself joyful be- | fore the | Lord, the | king.

8 Let the sea make a noise, and all that | there-in | is; ‖ the round world, and | they that | dwell there- | in.

9 Let the floods clap their hands, and let the hills be joyful together be- | fore the | Lord; ‖ for he | cometh ·· to | judge the | earth.

10 With righteousness shall he | judge the | world, ‖ and the | peo-ple | with— | equity.

Glory be to the Father, and | to the | Son, ‖ and | to the | Ho-ly | Ghost;

As it was in the beginning, is now, and | ever ·· shall | be, ‖ world | with-out | end. A- | men.

No. 4.

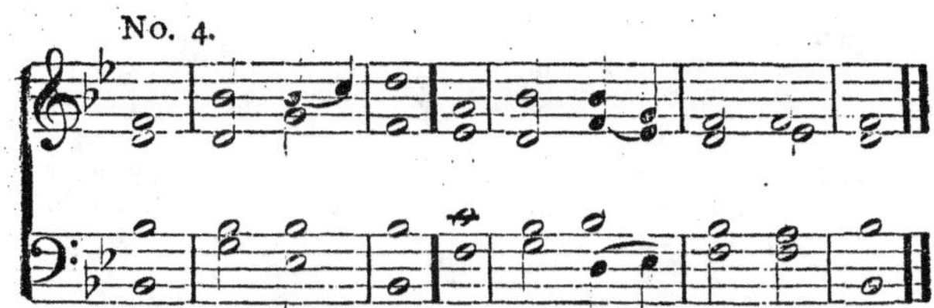

PSALM XIX.

1 The heavens declare the glory of God; and the firmament sheweth his | han .. dy- | work. ||

2 Day unto day uttereth speech, and | night unto .. night | shew-eth | knowledge.

3 There is no speech nor language, where their | voice .. is not | heard ||

4 Their line is gone out through all the earth, and their | words .. to the | end .. of the | world.

5 In them hath he set a tabernacle for the sun, which is as a bridegroom coming out of his chamber, and rejoiceth as a strong man to | run a | race. ||

6 His going forth is from the end of the heaven, and his circuit unto the ends of it: and there is nothing | hid .. from the | heat there- | of.

7 The law of the Lord is perfect, con- | verting .. the | soul: || the testimony of the Lord is | sure, .. making | wise the | simple.

8 The statutes of the Lord are right, re- | joicing .. the | heart: || the commandment of the Lord is | pure, en- | lightening .. the | eyes.

9 The fear of the Lord is clean, en- | during .. for | ever: || the judgments of the Lord are | true and | righteous .. alto- | gether.

10 More to be desired are they than gold, yea, than much fine gold: sweeter also than honey, and the | hon-ey- | comb. ||

11 Moreover by them is thy servant warned: and in keeping of | them, .. there is | great re- | ward.

12 Who can under- | stand his | errors? || cleanse thou | me from | se-cret | faults.

13 Keep back thy servant also from presumptuous sins; let them not have do- | min-ion | over me: ‖ then shall I be upright, and I shall be innocent | from the | great trans- | gression.

14 Let the words of my mouth, and the meditation of my heart be acceptable | in thy | sight, ‖ O Lord, my | strength, and | my re- | deemer.

LUKE II.

1 There were shepherds abiding in the field, keeping watch over their | flock by | night.

2 And lo, the angel of the Lord came upon them, and the glory of the Lord shone round about them, and | they were | sore a- | fraid.

3 And the angel said unto them, Fear not; for behold, I bring you good tidings of great joy, which shall be to | all= | people.

4 For unto you is born this day, in the city of David, a | Saviour, ·· who is | Christ the | Lord.

5 And suddenly there was with the angel, a multitude of the heavenly host, praising | God, and | saying:

6 Glory to God in the highest, and on earth | peace, good | will to | men.

No. 5.

PRAISE THE LORD—PSALM CIII.

1 Praise the Lord, | O my | soul ;‖ and all that is within me, | praise his | ho-ly | name.
2 Praise the Lord, | O my | soul ;‖ and for- | get not | all his | benefits.

3 Who forgiveth | all thy | sin, ‖ and healeth | all— | thine in- | firmities :
4 Who saveth thy life | from de- | struction, ‖ and crowneth thee with | mercy ·· and | lov-ing- | kindness.

5 O praise the Lord, ye angels of his, ye that ex- | cel in | strength ; ‖ ye that fulfill his commandment, and hearken unto the | voice— | of his | word.
6 O praise the Lord, all | ye his | hosts ; ‖ ye servants of | his that | do his | pleasure.

7 O speak good of the Lord, all ye works of his, in all places of | his do- | minion : ‖ Praise thou the | Lord,— | O my | soul.

No. 6.

BLESSED BE THE LORD.

1 Blessed be the Lord | God of | Israel, ‖ for he hath visited, | and re- | deemed his | people ;

2 And hath raised up a mighty sal- | va - tion | for us ‖ in the | house ·· of his | ser - vant | David :

3 As he spake by the mouth of his | ho - ly | prophets, ‖ which have been | since the | world be- | gan ,

4 That we should be saved | from our | enemies ‖ and from the | hand of | all that | hate us.

Glory be to the Father, and | to the | Son, ‖ and | to the | Ho - ly | Ghost ,

As it was in the beginning, is now, and | ever ·· shall | be, ‖ world | with - out | end. A- | men.

No. 7.

OH COME, LET US SING.—PSALM XCV.

1 Oh come, let us sing un- | to the | Lord, ‖ let us heartily rejoice in the | strength of | our sal- | vation

2 Let us come before his presence | with thanks- | giving ‖ and show ourselves | glad in | him with | psalms.

3 For the Lord is a | great— | God, ‖ and a great | King a- | bove all | gods.

4 In his hand are all the corners | of the | earth; || and the strength of the | hills is | his═ | also.

5 The sea is his, | and he | made it; || and his hands pre- | pared the | dry═ | land.

6 Oh come, let us worship | and fall | down, || and kneel be- | fore the | Lord our | Maker.

7 For he is the | Lord our | God, || and we are people of his pasture, and the | sheep of | his═ | hand.

8 Oh worship the Lord in the | beauty ·· of | holiness; || let the whole earth | stand in | awe of | him.

9 For he cometh, for he cometh to | judge the | earth; || and with righteousness to judge the world, and the | peo-ple | with his | truth.

Glory be to the Father, and | to the | Son, || and | to the | Ho-ly | Ghost;
As it was in the beginning, is now, and | ever ·· shall | be; || world | with-out | end. A- | men.

No. 8.

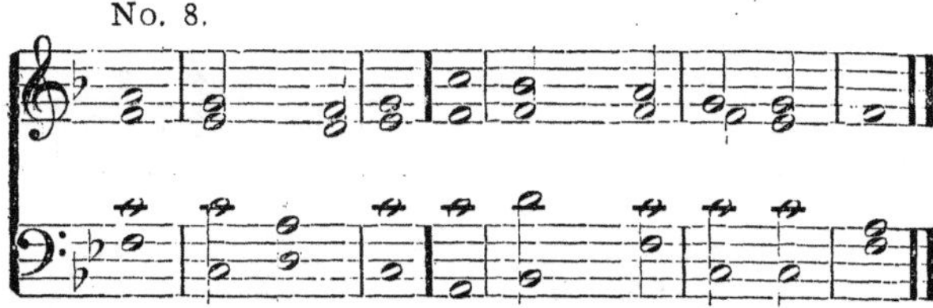

THE LORD IS MY SHEPHERD.—PSALM XXIII.

1 The Lord is my shepherd; I | shall not | want. || He maketh me to lie down in green pastures; he leadeth me be- | side the | still═ | waters.

2 He restoreth my soul; he leadeth me in the paths of righteousness for his | name's═ | sake. || Yea, though I walk through the valley of the shadow of death, I will fear no evil: for thou art with me; thy rod and thy | staff they | com-fort | me.

3 Thou preparest a table before me in the presence of mine enemies, thou anointest my head with oil: my | cup ·· runneth | over. || Surely goodness and mercy shall follow me all the days of my life; and I will dwell in the house of the | Lord, for | ever. ·· A- | men.

THE INVITATION.

1 Come unto me all ye that labor and are | hea-vy | laden, ‖ and | I will | give you | rest.

2 Take my yoke upon you, and learn of me ; for I am meek and | lowly ·· in | heart : ‖ and ye shall find | rest un- | to your | souls.

3 For my yoke is easy, and my | burden ·· is | light, ‖ For my yoke is easy, | and my | burden ·· is | light.

4 And the Spirit and the bride say, come. And let him that | heareth ·· say, | come. ‖ And let him that is athirst come ; and whosoever will, let him take the | water ·· of | life═ | freely.

No. 9.

GOD BE MERCIFUL.—PSALM LXVII.

1 God be merciful unto | us, and | bless us, ‖ and show us the light of his countenance, and be | mer-ci- | ful un- | to us.

2 That thy way may be | known ·· upon | earth, ‖ thy saving | health a- | mong all | nations.

3 Let the people praise | thee, O | God : ‖ yea, let | all the | peo-ple | praise thee.

4 Oh let the nations rejoice | and be | glad, ‖ for thou shalt judge the folk righteously, and govern the | na-tions | up-on | earth.

5 Let the people praise | thee, O | God: ‖ yea, let | all the | peo-ple | praise thee.

6 Then shall the earth bring | forth her | increase: ‖ and God, even our own | God shall | give us ·· his | blessing.

7 God— shall | bless us, ‖ and all the ends of the | world shall | fear— | him.

Glory be to the Father, and | to the | Son, ‖ and | to the | Ho-ly | Ghost;

As it was in the beginning, is now, and | ever ·· shall | be, ‖ world | with-out | end. A- | men.

No. 10.

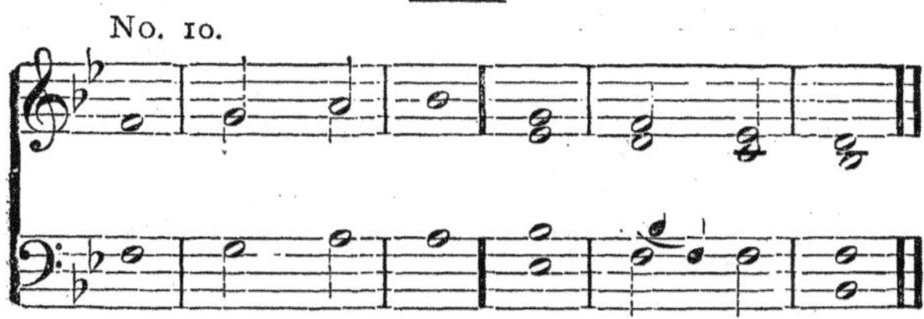

I WILL LIFT UP MINE EYES.—PSALM CXXI.

1 I will lift up mine eyes unto the hills, from whence | cometh ·· my | help. ‖

2 My help cometh from the Lord, which made | heaven ·· and | earth.

3 He will not suffer thy foot to be moved: he that keepeth thee | will not | slumber. ‖

4 Behold, he that keepeth Israel shall neither | slumber ·· nor | sleep.

5 The Lord is thy keeper: the Lord is thy shade upon thy | right— | hand, ‖

6 The sun shall not smite thee by day, nor the | moon by | night.

7 The Lord shall preserve thee from all evil: he shall pre- | serve thy | soul. ‖

8 The Lord shall preserve thy going out and thy coming in, from this time forth, and even for ever more. | A— | men.

"Happy Home."
S. H. Dyer.
ff
p
1. A cit - y bright and fair By faith I see, Far in the heaven-ly air Pre-pared for me. But in its gol-den street, None but the good shall meet— Dear
2. A bright and glo-rious crown, By faith I see, Safe in the Sav-iour's hand, Pre-pared for me. From sin and fol-ly's ways, Lord, guide me all my days— Je-
3. A robe of pur - est white By faith I see, Made for the saints in light, Pre-pared for me. To learn thy will di-vine, Give me a wil - ling mind, That
4. A home in heaven a-bove By faith I see— To-ken of Je - sus' love, Pre-pared for me. Dear Sav-iour, guide my feet, In - to that safe re-treat, Where

"Happy Home."—*Concluded.*

www.ingramcontent.com/pod-product-compliance
Lightning Source LLC
LaVergne TN
LVHW010236110826
845151LV00004B/1311

* 9 7 8 1 4 2 5 5 2 5 0 1 9 *